PRACTICE MAKES PERFECT®

Spanish Vocabulary Games

Gilda Nissenberg, PhD

Mc
Graw
Hill
Education

New York   Chicago   San Francisco   Athens   London   Madrid
Mexico City   Milan   New Delhi   Singapore   Sydney   Toronto

6 7 8 9 10 11 QVS/QVS 21 20 19 18 17

ISBN   978-0-07-182787-4
MHID   0-07-182787-0

Library of Congress Control Number 2013947033

McGraw-Hill Education, the McGraw-Hill Education logo, Practice Makes
Perfect, and related trade dress are trademarks or registered trademarks of
McGraw-Hill Education and/or its affiliates in the United States and other
countries and may not be used without written permission. All other trademarks
are the property of their respective owners. McGraw-Hill Education is not
associated with any product or vendor mentioned in this book.

McGraw-Hill Education products are available at special quantity discounts
to use as premiums and sales promotions or for use in corporate training
programs. To contact a representative, please visit the Contact Us pages at
www.mhprofessional.com.

This book is printed on acid-free paper.

Also by Gilda Nissenberg

Practice Makes Perfect: Complete Spanish Grammar
Practice Makes Perfect: Intermediate Spanish Grammar
Practice Makes Perfect: Spanish Sentence Builder
Must-Know Spanish

Contents

Introduction

Practice Makes Perfect: Spanish Vocabulary Games contains a collection of vocabulary puzzles and other fun word games organized into thematic units constructed around lists of important vocabulary. These vocabulary lists range in difficulty from advanced beginner to intermediate, and taken together they encompass more than a thousand words. Students and independent learners of Spanish can learn or review vocabulary items in an enjoyable and motivating way. And Spanish teachers, whether they are introducing new vocabulary or reviewing vocabulary already taught in class, can supplement their lessons with their favorite games from this book. **¡Aprender español es muy divertido!**

Each unit begins with extensive, themed vocabulary lists. You can study these lists or, better, simply refer back to them as a reference for those puzzles that prove to be challenging. The vocabulary games you'll encounter are word searches, crosswords (**crucigramas**), acrostics, scrambles, and more. At the beginning of most units, you'll also find a game of **cognados**—cognates. Here, you'll discover Spanish words very similar to English ones. These **cognados** will form another vocabulary list.

It is best for the learner to resist the temptation to start by skimming through the lists: it will be much more fun if you test your skills first and resort to the lists only to fill in any gaps that become apparent. Note that vocabulary items are often used in more than one game, which reinforces your grasp of them.

Hints for solving the puzzles:

1. In the puzzles, the spaces are omitted from compound expressions or phrases such as **la puerta de embarque** (*gate*).

2. Be sure to recognize and distinguish among nouns, adjectives, verbs, and adverbs. When dealing with nouns and adjectives, be sure to understand their gender and number. For example, if the clue is: *bank teller* (*f*), make sure to write **cajera** (for a female bank teller) and not **cajero**.

3. Use a pencil. Just because a word fits a particular blank doesn't mean it is necessarily the right answer, and you may need to make corrections to what you have written as you look for the answers that will work to solve the puzzle as a whole. If you are having trouble, go back and review the vocabulary lists. As a last resort, the answers to the games are provided in the back of the book.

4. Most of all, have fun! These games are meant to be an entertaining source of vocabulary review.

Las comunicaciones y los medios

Communications and media

VOCABULARIO

Communications	Las comunicaciones
acquaintance	el conocido, la conocida
delighted	encantado, -a
farewell	hasta luego; despedida
first name	el nombre
glad	alegre; contento, -a
to greet	saludar
greeting	el saludo
hello	hola
last name	el apellido
to meet	conocer
to say good-bye	despedirse
you are welcome	de nada

Communication by phone	La comunicación por teléfono
to answer	responder
to call	llamar; llamar por teléfono
cell phone	el celular; el móvil
to dial	marcar
to hang up	colgar el teléfono
Hello	¡Diga!; ¡Oigo!
to leave a message	dejar un mensaje
message	el mensaje; el recado; el mensaje electrónico
to phone	llamar por teléfono; telefonear
to reply	contestar; responder
telephone number	el número de teléfono
wrong number	el número equivocado

Letters	Las cartas
address	la dirección
airmail	el correo aéreo
date	la fecha
envelope	el sobre
letter	la carta
mail	el correo
mailbox	el buzón
postal carrier	el cartero, la cartera
recipient	el destinatario, la destinataria
sender	el/la remitente

Letters (cont.)

signature	la firma
stamp	la estampilla; el sello
zip code	el código postal, el código

Computers and electronic mail

to access	acceder
archive	el archivo
browser	el navegador
to charge	cargar
charger	el cargador
chat (noun)	el chat
to chat	chatear
chip	el chip de la computadora
computer	la computadora
computer game	el videojuego
computer virus	el virus
to delete	eliminar
e-mail	e-mail
to hack	hackear; piratear
hacker	el pirata informático; el/la hacker
identity	la identidad
key	la tecla
keyboard	el teclado
landing page	la página inicial
laptop	el laptop
memory stick	la memoria USB
monitor	el monitor
mouse	el ratón
password	la contraseña
to pirate	piratear; hackear
to plug in	enchufar
printer	la impresora
to scan	escanear
scanner	el escáner
screen	la pantalla
user	el usuario, la usuaria
web page	la página de la web

Newspapers and magazines

ad	el anuncio
article	el artículo
blog	el blog
blogger	el bloguero, la bloguera
business section	las finanzas
column	la columna
crossword puzzle	el crucigrama
cuisine	la gastronomía
entertaining	el entretenimiento
front page	la portada

Newspapers and magazines (cont.)   Los periódicos y las revistas (cont.)

headline	el titular
horoscope	el horóscopo
magazine	la revista
media	los medios
movie section	la cartelera
news	las noticias
press	la prensa
program	el programa
to publish	publicar
puzzle	el puzle
to read	leer
reporter	el reportero, la reportera
short story	el cuento
sports section	los deportes
travel section	los viajes

Radio and television   La radio y la televisión

alert	la alerta
cable	el cable
cartoon	el dibujo animado
channel	el canal de la tele
character	el personaje
comedy	la comedia
documentary	el documental
episode	el episodio
mystery show	el programa de suspenso
news alert, breaking news	las noticias de última hora
radio listener	el/la radioyente
radio station	la emisora
to register	registrarse
remote control	el control remoto
satellite	el satélite
soap opera	la telenovela
television program	el programa de televisión
trashy TV	la telebasura
TV set	el televisor; la tele
TV viewer	el/la televidente
weather report	el reporte del tiempo

Movies and the theater   El cine y el teatro

act (noun)	la actuación
to act	actuar
to applaud	aplaudir
applause	el aplauso
audience	la audiencia
award	el premio
cinematography	la cinematografía
climax	el clímax
drama	el drama

Movies and the theater (cont.)	El cine y el teatro (cont.)
dramatic	dramático, -a
dubbed	doblado, -a
ending	el final
exciting	emocionante
film/movie	el film; la película
to film	filmar
flop	el fracaso
funny	chistoso, -a; cómico, -a
movie star	la estrella de cine
moving	conmovedor, conmovedora
play	la obra de teatro
plot	el argumento; la trama
premiere	el estreno
rehearsal	el ensayo
to rehearse	ensayar
role	el papel
scene	la escena
stage	el escenario
subtitle	el subtítulo
success	el éxito
ticket	el billete; la entrada
tragic	trágico, -a
usher	el acomodador, la acomodadora

Saludos y despedidas. *Translate from English into Spanish.*

1. greetings ___el saludo___
2. farewell ___hasta luego; despedida___
3. to meet ___conocer___
4. good-bye ___despedirse___
5. to answer ___responder___
6. thanks ___gracias___
7. you are welcome ___de nada___
8. to greet ___saludar___
9. address ___la dir___
10. glad ___alegre; contento, -a___

Cognados. *Translate these words from English into Spanish and use the articles **el, la, los,** and **las** as necessary.*

1. to act ___actuar___
2. computer chip (*m.*) ___el chip de la computadora___
3. computer virus (*m.*) ___el virus___
4. identity (*f.*) ___la identidad___
5. to hack ___hackear; piratear___
6. to delete ___eliminar___
7. dramatic ___dramático, -a___
8. to scan ___escanear___
9. blogger (*m./f.*) ___el bloguero, la bloguera___
10. hacker (*m.*) ___el pirata informático; el/la hacker___
11. puzzle (*m.*) ___el puzle___
12. chat (*m.*) ___el chat___
13. climax (*m.*) ___el clímax___
14. scene (*f.*) ___la escena___

15. suspense (m.) _____ el suspenso _____
16. alert (f.) _____ la alerta _____
17. television (f.) _____ la tele _____
18. horoscope (m.) _____ el horóscopo _____
19. film (m.) _____ filmar _____
20. comedy (f.) _____ la comedia _____
21. to publish _____ publicar _____
22. episode (m.) _____ el episodio _____
23. press (f.) _____ la prensa _____
24. satellite (m.) _____ el satélite _____
25. web page (f.) _____ la página de la web _____

JUEGO
1·3

La comunicación electrónica. *Provide the word or phrase that corresponds to each definition.*

1. La primera página de un sitio de Internet. _____ website _____

2. Tener entrada en una página de Internet. _____ accedar _____

3. Un aparato usando una mano humana para mover el cursor por la pantalla. _____
   _____ el ratón _____

4. Un lugar en la computadora para recordar (remember) algunas cosas. _____
   _____ el archivo _____

5. Lo que permite acceder a un lugar en la Internet. _____ la contraseña _____

6. Un programa que destruye la información, la memoria de la computadora. _____
   _____ el virus _____

7. Copiar fotos o documentos y poner las copias en la computadora. _____
   _____ la impresora _____

8. Un mensaje para amigos en la Internet. _____ el recado _____

9. Lo que contiene la pantalla de la computadora. _____

Palabras escondidas en este juego de puzle. *Find and circle the Spanish equivalents of these words hidden vertically, horizontally, and diagonally.*

```
M P N H I A G S K U M P E A P
S U A R A M K T V D S J J W E
M S O N L L A M A R A D I C T
A T Z W T C K L O S P Y T O G
R L B R F A Q B N I I E N N H
C O L G A R L E I V G K E T B
A M S W V G M L K A G O L R U
R N M H B A N U A C V R É A Z
F L N S B R H O R F P Q F S Ó
F B J U X N R I Z G X M O E N
P G P V B E K M Ó V I L N Ñ E
G L K C M G V I D N B C O A Z
A R N Ú P A C C E D E R C K J
T P N H L L F Z W C Ó D I G O
R E S P O N D E R D I W A C F
```

to access *accedar*	to dial	number
to answer *Responder*	to hang up	password
to call	hello	screen
cell phone	mailbox	telephone
to charge *cargar*	message *mensaje*	zip code

El sobre y la carta. *Translate the parts of the envelope and letter.*

1. {

2. Srta. Mila G. Salazar
123 José Bolivar
Los Angeles, CA 33010

3. [stamp]

4. Dr. Paula M. Juárez
5. 10013 José Martí.
6. Hollywood, CA 33010

8. 10 de noviembre, 2016

November 10, 2016

9. Querida Paula:

Dear Paula

10. Con un abrazo fuerte,

7. {

With a strong hug

11. Mila

Mine

1. envelope *el sobre*
2. sender *el remitente*
3. stamp *estampilla*
4. recipient *el destinatario*
5. address *la dirección*
6. zip code *el código*

7. letter *carta*
8. date *la fecha*
9. greeting *el saludo*
10. farewell *despedida*
11. signature *la firma*

Selección múltiple. *Choose the best response or ending for each statement.*

1. Yo escucho noticias en español en mi casa. Esa señora
   - (a) trabaja en una emisora hispana.
   - b. toca una guitarra.
   - c. presenta dibujos animados.
   - d. usa el control remoto.

2. Hace frío y antes de salir de casa, yo veo en la tele
   - a. el programa ausente.
   - (b) el reporte del tiempo.
   - c. la contraseña.
   - d. la fecha.

3. Uso mi laptop para leer un periódico para ver mi futuro. Leo
   - (a) la edición impresa.
   - b. la sección de salud.
   - c. el horóscopo.
   - d. el blog.

4. Quiero ganar dinero y veo un canal de
   - (a) entretenimiento.
   - b. deportes.
   - c. finanzas.
   - d. películas.

5. A los niños les gusta ver esos programas:
   - a. los dibujos animados.
   - b. las telenovelas tontas.
   - c. las películas para adultos.
   - (d) los problemas económicos.

Palabras aprendidas. *Translate these words from English into Spanish. Reading down the highlighted letters will then reveal a Spanish word.*

1. postal carrier Cartero
2. hello hola
3. stamp estampilla
4. greeting saludo
5. name nombre
6. farewell despedida
7. to hang up colgar
8. message recado
9. acquainted conocido
10. last name appelido
11. mailbox buzon
12. you're welcome de nada

La palabra vertical: Comunicación

Un juego de palabras. *For each category below, choose the word or phrase that does **not** belong.*

1. **obras literarias con personajes** ~~el poema~~, el drama, la comedia, la telenovela

2. **los tipos de programas en la TV** las noticias, el horror, ~~el acomodador~~, las películas

3. **las secciones de los periódicos** la cartelera, los viajes, ~~los cómicos~~, el radioyente

4. **las reacciones a malas noticias** tener miedo, estar triste, ~~estar feliz~~, tener ansiedad

5. **las partes de la computadora** la pantalla, ~~la cucaracha~~, el chip, el ratón

6. **los programas de la radio** las noticias del día, la música, el diálogo con el radioyente, ~~el dibujo animado~~

7. **las reacciones a una comedia de TV** reír, ~~llorar~~, sonreír, estar contento

8. **los elementos de las cartas** la fecha, el mensaje, ~~la pantalla~~, la firma

9. **las partes de la carta** ~~el chip~~, el apellido, la dirección, el código postal

10. **las secciones de revistas** la foto, la portada, ~~la gramática~~, la moda

Un juego acróstico. *Translate the clues on the left from English into Spanish. Reading down the first letter of each word will then reveal a Spanish word.*

1. short story   Cuento
2. magazine   Revista
3. user (*m.*)   Usuari
4. column   Columna
5. Internet   Internet
6. cuisine   Gastronomía
7. reporter (*f.*)   Repertero
8. ad   Anunci
9. media   Medio
10. article   Artículo

La palabra vertical: Crucigrama

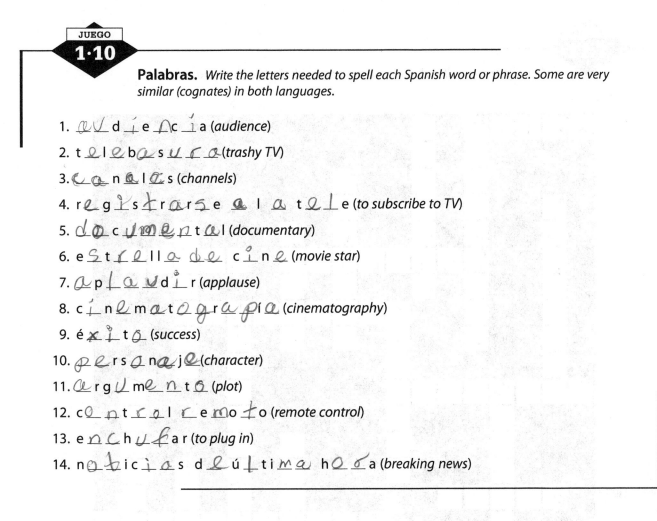

JUEGO 1·10

Palabras. *Write the letters needed to spell each Spanish word or phrase. Some are very similar (cognates) in both languages.*

1. au d i e n c i a (*audience*)
2. t e l e b a s u r a (*trashy TV*)
3. c a n a l a s (*channels*)
4. r e g i s t r a r s e a l a t e l e (*to subscribe to TV*)
5. d o c u m e n t a l (*documentary*)
6. e s t r e l l a d e c i n e (*movie star*)
7. a p l a u d i r (*applause*)
8. c i n e m a t o g r a f i a (*cinematography*)
9. é x i t o (*success*)
10. p e r s o n a j e (*character*)
11. a r g u m e n t o (*plot*)
12. c o n t r o l r e m o t o (*remote control*)
13. e n c h u f a r (*to plug in*)
14. n o t i c i a s d e ú l ti m a h o r a (*breaking news*)

Crucigrama. *Fill in the crossword puzzle with the Spanish words.*

Horizontales (*Across*)

1. drama
8. movie star
9. ending

10. audience
12. screen
17. success

18. exciting
19. funny (*f.*)

Verticales (*Down*)

2. plot
3. ticket
4. dubbed (*m.*)
5. movie

6. role
7. rehearsal
10. applause
11. moving (*m.*)

13. tragic (*m.*)
14. subtitle
15. flop
16. theater

De la vida humana: las relaciones, las celebraciones y las nacionalidades

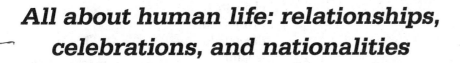

All about human life: relationships, celebrations, and nationalities

VOCABULARIO	
Friendship and personality	**La amistad y la personalidad**
charming	encantador, encantadora
courageous	valiente
cowardly	cobarde
creative	creativo, -a
cute	bello, -a
discreet	discreto, -a
dishonest	deshonesto, -a
energetic	enérgico, -a
extroverted	extrovertido, -a
faithful	fiel
friend	el amigo, la amiga
friendship	la amistad
handy	habilidoso, -a
happy	feliz
hardworking	trabajador, trabajadora
honest	honesto, -a
lazy	vago, -a
loyal	leal
nice	amable
offensive	insultante
persevering	perseverante
playful	juguetón, juguetona
pleasant	simpático, -a
quiet	callado, -a
resourceful	ingenioso, -a; emprendedor, emprendedora
rough	brusco, -a
rude	descarado, -a
shrewd	astuto, -a
trait	el rasgo
unfaithful	infiel
unpleasant	antipático, -a
wise	sabio, -a

Family relations

to adopt	adoptar
adopted	adoptado, -a
aunt	la tía
brother	el hermano
daughter	la hija
daughter-in-law	la nuera
divorce (noun)	el divorcio
to divorce	divorciarse
divorced	divorciado, -a
family	la familia
father	el padre
father-in-law	el suegro
female cousin	la prima
fiancé	el prometido
fiancée	la prometida
godfather	el padrino
godmother	la madrina
godparents	los padrinos
granddaughter	la nieta
grandfather	el abuelo
grandmother	la abuela
grandparents	los abuelos
grandson	el nieto
husband	el esposo; el marido
in-laws	la familia política
male cousin	el primo
mother	la madre
mother-in-law	la suegra
nephew	el sobrino
niece	la sobrina
oldest child	el hijo mayor, la hija mayor
only child	el hijo único, la hija única
relative	el/la pariente
sister	la hermana
son	el hijo
son-in-law	el yerno
stepdaughter	la hijastra
stepfather	el padrastro
stepmother	la madrastra
stepson	el hijastro
uncle	el tío
wife	la esposa; la mujer
youngest child	el hijo menor, la hija menor

Las relaciones familiares

Celebrations and traditions

birth	el nacimiento
birthday	el cumpleaños
bread pudding	el budín de pan
cake	el pastel; la torta
candles	las velitas
to celebrate	celebrar; festejar

Las celebraciones y las tradiciones

Celebrations and traditions (cont.)

champagne	el champán
christening	el bautismo
Christmas	la Navidad, las Navidades
Christmas Eve	la Nochebuena
confetti	el confeti
confidence	la confianza
engaged: to get engaged	comprometerse
engagement	el compromiso; el noviazgo
engagement ring	el anillo de compromiso
event	el acontecimiento
Father's Day	el Día del Padre
fireworks	los juegos artificiales
Halloween	la Noche de las Brujas
Independence Day	el Día de la Independencia
marriage	el matrimonio
married: to get married	casarse
mass	la misa
Mother's Day	el Día de la Madre
New Year's Day	el Año Nuevo
New Year's Eve	la Nochevieja
party	la fiesta
piñata	la piñata
Ramadan	el Ramadán
red wine	el vino tinto
relationship	la relación
rice pudding	el arroz con leche
Thanksgiving	el Día de Gracias
tradition	la tradición
Valentine's Day	el Día de San Valentín; el Día de la Amistad; el Día del Amor
to visit	visitar
wedding	la boda
wedding anniversary	el aniversario de boda
white wine	el vino blanco
wine	el vino

Nationalities and places of origin

Africa

African	africano, -a; del continente de África
Algerian	algerino, -a; de Algeria
Angolan	angoleño, -a; de República de la Angola
Egyptian	egipcio, -a; de Egipto
Ethiopian	etíope; de Etiopía
Libyan	libio, -a; de Libia
Moroccan	marroquí; de Marruecos
Mozambican	mozambiqueño, -a; de Mozambique
South African	surafricano, -a; de Sur África
Sudanese	sudanés; de Sudán
Tanzanian	tanzano, -a; de Tanzania
Tunisian	tunecino, -a; de la República Tunecina

Las celebraciones y las tradiciones (cont.)

Las nacionalidades y los lugares de origen

África

The Americas: North America, Central America, and South America	Las Américas: América del Norte, América Central y América del Sur
American	americano, -a; estadounidense; de los Estados Unidos
Argentine, Argentinean	argentino, -a; de Argentina
Bolivian	boliviano, -a; de Bolivia
Brazilian	brasilero, -a; brasileño, -a; de Brasil
Canadian	canadiense; de Canadá
Caribbean	caribeño, -a; del Caribe
Chilean	chileno, -a; de Chile
Colombian	colombiano, -a; de Colombia
Costa Rican	costarricense; de Costa Rica
Cuban	cubano, -a; de Cuba
Dominican	dominicano, -a; de la República Dominicana
Ecuadorian	ecuatoriano, -a; de Ecuador
Guatemalan	guatemalteco, -a; de Guatemala
Haitian	haitiano, -a; de Haití
Hawaiian	hawaiano, -a; de Hawái
Honduran	hondureño, -a; de Honduras
Mexican	mexicano, -a; de México
Nicaraguan	nicaragüense; de Nicaragua
Panamanian	panameño, a; de Panamá
Paraguayan	paraguayo, -a; de Paraguay
Peruvian	peruano, -a; de Perú
Puerto Rican	puertorriqueño, -a; de Puerto Rico
Salvadoran	salvadoreño, -a; de El Salvador
Uruguayan	uruguayo, -a; de Uruguay
Venezuelan	venezolano, -a; de Venezuela

Asia and the Middle East	Asia y el Oriente Medio
Afghani	afgano, -a; de Afganistán
Asian	asiático, -a; del continente de Asia
Chinese	chino, -a; de la República Popular China
Hindu	hindú; indio, -a; de la India
Indonesian	indonesio, -a; de Indonesia
Iranian	iraní; de Irán
Iraqi	iraquí; de Iraq
Israeli	israelita, israelí; de Israel
Japanese	japonés, japonesa; de Japón
Korean	coreano, -a; de Corea, Corea del Norte o Corea del Sur
Lebanese	libanés, libanesa; del Líbano
Pakistani	pakistaní; de Pakistán
Palestinian	palestino, -a; de Palestina
Filipino, Filipina	filipino, -a; de las Filipinas
Saudi Arabian	saudí; de Arabia Saudí
Vietnamese	vietnamita; de Vietnam
Yemeni	yemení; de Yemen

Oceania	Oceanía
Australian	australiano, -a
Easter Islander	de Isla de Pascua
New Zealander	neozelandés, neozelandesa; de Nuevo Zelanda

Europe	Europa
Belgian	bélgico, -a; de Bélgica
British	británico, -a; de Inglaterra
Danish	danés, danesa; de Dinamarca
Dutch	holandés, holandesa; de Holanda
Estonian	estoniano, -a; de Estonia
European	europeo, -a; del continente de Europa
Finnish	finlandés, finlandesa; de Finlandia
French	francés, francesa; de Francia
German	alemán, alemana; de Alemania
Greek	griego, -a; de Grecia
Hungarian	húngaro, -a; de Hungría
Icelandic	islandés, islandesa; de Islandia
Irish	irlandés, irlandesa; de Irlanda
Italian	italiano, -a; de Italia
Norwegian	noruego, -a; de Noruega
Polish	polaco, -a; de Polonia
Portuguese	portugués, portuguesa; de Portugal
Romanian	rumano, -a; de Rumania
Russian	ruso, -a; de Rusia
Spanish	español, española; de España
Swedish	sueco, -a; de Suecia
Swiss	suizo, -a; de Suiza
Turkish	turco, -a; de Turquía
Ukrainian	ucraniano, -a; de Ucrania
Welsh	gales, galesa: de Gales

Ethnicity and religion — Los étnicos y la religión

atheism	el ateísmo
Buddhism	el budismo
Buddhist (adj.)	budista
Catholic (adj.)	católico, -a
Catholicism	el catolicismo
Christian (adj.)	cristiano, -a
Christianity	la cristiandad
ethnic	étnico, -a
Hispanic (adj.)	hispano, -a
Islam	el islamismo
Jewish	judío, -a
Judaism	el judaísmo
Muslim (adj.)	musulmán, musulmana; islamita
prejudice	el prejuicio
Protestant (adj.)	protestante
Protestantism	el protestantismo
racism	el racismo
religion	la religión
religious	religioso, -a

Languages — Los lenguajes

Arabic	el árabe
Asian languages	las lenguas asiáticas
Basque	el vasco; el vascuence

Languages (cont.)	Los lenguajes (cont.)
Catalonian	el catalán
Chinese	el chino
Danish	el danés
Dutch	el holandés
English	el inglés
Euskera (= Basque)	el vasco; el vascuence
Finnish	el finlandés
French	el francés
German	el alemán
Italian	el italiano
Japanese	el japonés
Latin	el latín
Mandarin	el mandarín
Norwegian	el noruego
Polish	el polaco
Portuguese	el portugués
Russian	el ruso
Spanish	el español
Swedish	el sueco
Vietnamese	el vietnamita

JUEGO 2·1

Descripciones de las personalidades. *What adjective would you use to describe each of the following? (Note: some are singular and some are plural.)*

1. Una señora que no tiene paciencia ____impatient____

2. Persona que tiene muchas emociones ____emotional____

3. Un escritor como Cervantes, autor de *Don Quijote* _____

4. Un chico que no comparte sus ideas, sus sentimientos con otras personas _____

_____

5. Una chica que habla la verdad ____truthful____

6. Comentario absurdo _____

7. Persona que tiene muchos amigos ____fullfit____

8. Comentario imprudente _____

9. Persona que tiene muchos conocimientos ____famous____

10. Personas que están muy contentas ____excited____

11. Personas que se creen superiores a los demás _____

12. Un chico que tiene mucha paciencia _Patient_

13. Una persona que no es chistosa _Serious_

14. Opuesto a introvertido _____

Palabras escondidas en este juego de puzle. *Find and circle the Spanish words hidden vertically, horizontally, and diagonally.*

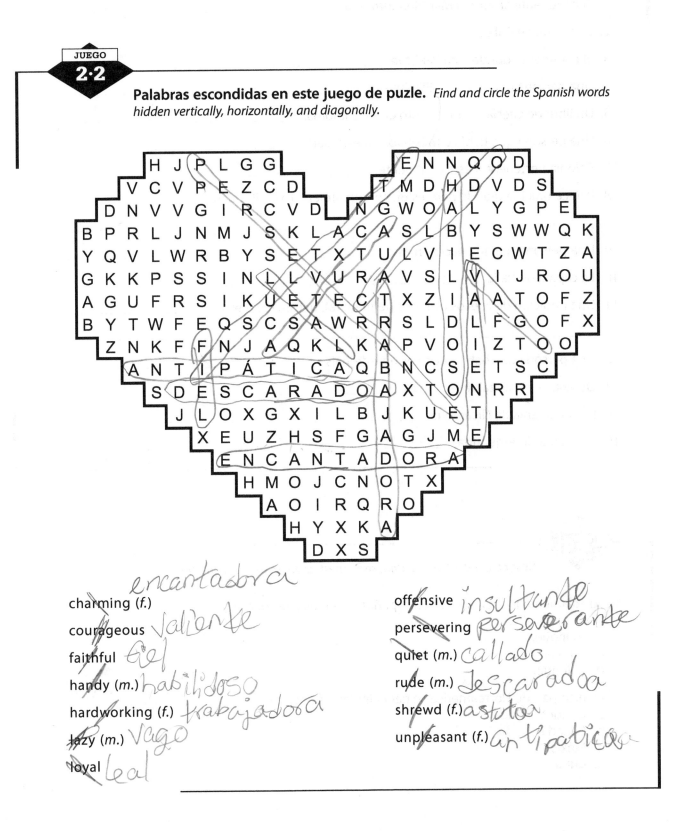

charming (f.) _encantadora_
courageous _valiente_
faithful _fiel_
handy (m.) _habilidoso_
hardworking (f.) _trabajadora_
lazy (m.) _vago_
loyal _leal_

offensive _insultante_
persevering _perseverante_
quiet (m.) _callado_
rude (m.) _descaradoa_
shrewd (f.) _astuta_
unpleasant (f.) _antipaticaa_

Palabras de nacionalidad, tradiciones y más. *Write the word or phrase in Spanish.*

1. El continente al sur del Mar Mediterráneo. _____

2. La capital de Cuba. _____

3. El continente donde está Pakistán. _____

4. Una persona que nació en Filipinas. _____

5. Un libro de Grecia estaría escrito en este idioma. _____

6. Una persona que habla danés nace en este país. _____

7. Polonia pertenece a este continente. _____

8. Parece una isla grande pero es un continente en el Mar Pacífico. _____

_____

9. Una persona rumana nació en este país. _____

10. La capital de Italia. ___Rome_____

11. Una tradición de zuecos (zapatos de madera), pertenece a este país. _____

_____

12. Una persona que habla sueco es de este país. _____

13. Ottawa es la capital de este país. _____

14. La ciudadanía de Nicaragua. _____

15. La capital de Argentina. ___Buenos Aires_____

Selección múltiple. *Choose the best response for each question.*

1. Yo solamente leo las noticias en español y en inglés porque soy
   a. monolingüe.
   b. trilingüe.
   c. multilingüe.
   d. bilingüe.

2. En este país de Norteamérica se habla inglés y francés.
   a. Estados Unidos
   b. Canadá
   c. México
   d. Cuba

3. El cumpleaños para los niños prefieren
   a. la ensalada.
   b. la boda.
   c. el vino.
   d. la piñata.

4. El Día del Año Nuevo hay tradiciones y
   a. se come el arroz con leche.
   b. se bebe champán.
   c. se come el desayuno.
   d. se bebe agua.

5. El adjetivo **étnico** tiene que ver con esta palabra:
   a. protestante.
   b. prejuicio.
   c. radical.
   d. alemán.

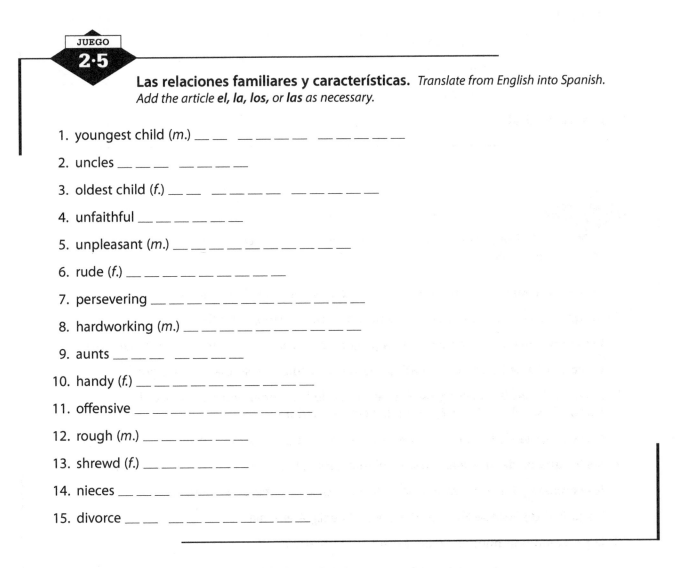

JUEGO

2·5

Las relaciones familiares y características. *Translate from English into Spanish.*
*Add the article **el, la, los,** or **las** as necessary.*

1. youngest child (*m.*) __ __ __ __ __ __ __ __ __ __ __ __ __

2. uncles __ __ __ __ __ __ __ __

3. oldest child (*f.*) __ __ __ __ __ __ __ __ __ __ __ __ __

4. unfaithful __ __ __ __ __ __ __

5. unpleasant (*m.*) __ __ __ __ __ __ __ __ __ __ __

6. rude (*f.*) __ __ __ __ __ __ __ __ __

7. persevering __ __ __ __ __ __ __ __ __ __ __ __

8. hardworking (*m.*) __ __ __ __ __ __ __ __ __ __ __

9. aunts __ __ __ __ __ __ __ __

10. handy (*f.*) __ __ __ __ __ __ __ __ __ __

11. offensive __ __ __ __ __ __ __ __ __ __ __

12. rough (*m.*) __ __ __ __ __ __ __

13. shrewd (*f.*) __ __ __ __ __ __ __

14. nieces __ __ __ __ __ __ __ __ __ __

15. divorce __ __ __ __ __ __ __ __ __ __ __

Palabras aprendidas. *Translate these words from English into Spanish. (Some words were introduced in this chapter; others you learned earlier.) Reading down the boxed column will then reveal a Spanish word or phrase.*

1. afternoon snack __ __ __ __ __ __ ▨ __

    2. breakfast __ __ __ __ __ ▨ __ __

      3. cake __ __ __ __ __ ▨

        4. dinner ▨ __ __ __

      5. cheese __ __ ▨ __ __ __

    6. bread pudding __ __ ▨ __ __ __ __ __ __ __

    7. meringue __ __ __ ▨ __ __ __ __

      8. lunch __ ▨ __ __ __ __ __ __

9. chocolate __ __ __ __ __ __ __ __ ▨

      10. coffee ▨ __ __ __

    11. champagne __ ▨ __ __ __ __ __

      12. drinks __ ▨ __ __ __ __

La palabra vertical: _____

Un juego de palabras. *For each category below, choose the word or phrase that does not belong.*

1. **las celebraciones religiosas** el bautismo, la ciudadanía, la boda, la misa

2. **los grupos religiosos** el ateo, el islamismo, el catolicismo, el budismo

3. **la manera en que se comunican las personas** abrazarse, saludarse, crearse, hablarse

4. **el elemento de buena personalidad** honesto, insultante, simpático, discreto

5. **las tradiciones de países y familiares** el Día de la Independencia, el anillo de compromiso, el Día de los Muertos, los emprendedores

6. **las relaciones de familia** la silla, el matrimonio, los primos, los bisabuelos

7. **los lenguajes de diferentes países** el mandarín, el coreano, el danés, el descarado

8. **las comidas y las bebidas** el vino tinto, el arroz con leche, el valiente, el pastel

9. **los países de Europa** Francia, Marruecos, Suecia, Alemania

10. **la personalidad humana** vago, valiente, tío, creativo

Vocabulario en español: las relaciones de familia. *Fill in the letters needed to complete each Spanish word or phrase.*

1. y _e_ r _n_ _o_ (son-in-law)
2. p _a_ r _i_ e _n_ t _e_ (relative)
3. _p_ r _i_ m _o_ (cousin [m.])
4. n _u_ e _r_ a (daughter-in-law)
5. _a_ b _u_ _e_ _l_ a _s_ (grandmothers)
6. p r _o_ m _e_ t _i_ d _a_ (fiancée [f.])
7. h _i_ j _a_ _s_ t _r_ o (stepson)
8. s _ _ _ g _ _ _ _ (mother-in-law)
9. _e_ s _p_ o _s_ _a_ (wife)
10. _a_ _d_ o _p_ _t_ a _r_ (to adopt)
11. p _a_ d r _a_ s _t_ _r_ _o_ (stepfather)
12. _a_ b _u_ _e_ l _o_ s (grandparents)
13. _n_ i _e_ t _o_ (grandson)
14. f _a_ m _i_ _l_ i a p o _l_ í t i _c_ a (in-laws)
15. p _a_ d r _i_ _n_ o (godfather)

La capital de los países y la moneda de los países: Juego de respuestas y preguntas. *Write a question for every answer given below. The first one has been done for you.*

1. Puerto Príncipe ¿Cuál es la capital de Haití?
2. Bogotá _____
3. Asunción _____
4. Santiago _____
5. Madrid _____
6. Londres _____
7. el dólar canadiense _____
8. euro _____
9. el dólar _____
10. la libra esterlina _____

Un juego acróstico. *Translate the clues on the left from English into Spanish. Reading down the first letter of each word will then reveal a Spanish word or phrase.*

1. Libyan (*m.*) ▦ __ __ __ __

2. Lebanese (*f.*) ▦ __ __ __ __ __ __ __

3. European (*m.*) ▦ __ __ __ __ __ __

4. Venezuelan (*f.*) ▦ __ __ __ __ __ __ __ __ __

5. Argentine (*m.*) ▦ __ __ __ __ __ __ __ __

6. Romanian (*f.*) ▦ __ __ __ __ __

7. Swedish (*m.*) ▦ __ __ __ __

8. Ecuadorian (*f.*) ▦ __ __ __ __ __ __ __ __ __

9. Belgian (*m.*) ▦ __ __ __ __ __ __

10. Irish (*f.*) ▦ __ __ __ __ __ __ __

11. Estonian (*m.*) ▦ __ __ __ __ __ __ __ __

12. Nicaraguan (*m./f.*) ▦ __ __ __ __ __ __ __ __ __ __

La palabra vertical: _____

JUEGO
2·11

Crucigrama. *Fill in the crossword puzzle with the Spanish words.*

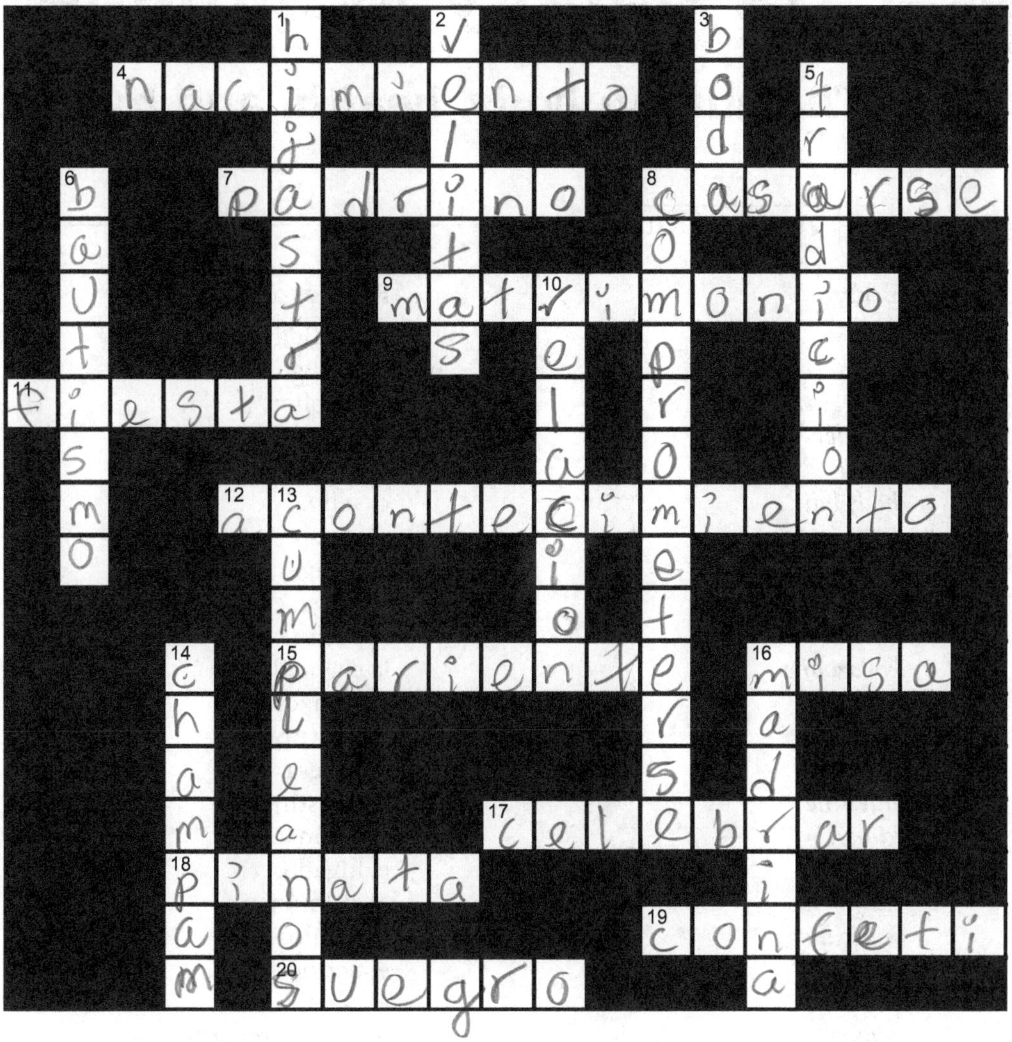

Horizontales (*Across*)

4. birth
7. godfather
8. to get married
9. marriage
11. party
12. event
15. relative
16. mass
17. to celebrate
18. piñata
19. confetti
20. father-in-law

Verticales (*Down*)

1. stepdaughter
2. candles
3. wedding
5. tradition
6. christening
8. to get engaged
10. relationship
13. birthday
14. champagne
16. godmother

El cuerpo humano, la salud y la higiene

The human body, health, and hygiene

Body	**El cuerpo**
back	la espalda
belly	la barriga; el vientre
belly button	el ombligo
bladder	la vejiga
blood	la sangre
body hair	el vello
bone	el hueso
bottom	las nalgas, el pompis
buttock	la nalga, el trasero
chest	el pecho
collarbone	la clavícula
heart	el corazón
height	la estatura
hip	la cadera
intestine	el intestino
kidney	el riñón
liver	el hígado
lung	el pulmón
muscular	musculoso, -a
nerve	el nervio
penis	el pene
plump	gordo, -a; regordete, -a
skeleton	el esqueleto
skin	la piel
skinny	flaco, -a
slender	delgado, -a
small	pequeño, -a
tall	alto, -a
torso	el torso
vagina	la vagina
vein	la vena
waist	la cintura
weight	el peso

Head and face	**La cabeza y la cara**
beard	la barba
brain	el cerebro
cheek	la mejilla; el cachete

Head and face (cont.)

chin	la barbilla; el mentón
collar	el cuello
complexion	el cutis, la piel
dark-skinned	moreno, -a
ear	la oreja
eye	el ojo
eyebrow	la ceja
eyelash	la pestaña
eyelid	el párpado
fair-skinned	de piel clara
forehead	la frente
freckle	la peca
freckled	pecoso, -a
jaw	la mandíbula; la quijada
lip	el labio
mole	el lunar
mustache	el bigote
nape	la nuca
neck	el cuello
nose	la nariz
pupil	la pupila (del ojo)
scar	la cicatriz
sideburn	la patilla
throat	la garganta
wrinkle	la arruga

Head and face (cont.) — La cabeza y la cara (cont.)

Hair — El pelo, el cabello

bald	calvo, -a
black hair	el pelo negro
blond, blonde	rubio, -a
curly hair	el pelo rizado
facial hair	el vello
gray hair	la cana
gray-haired	canoso, -a
red-haired	pelirrojo, -a
straight hair	el pelo lacio

Mouth — La boca

baby tooth	el diente de leche
canine tooth	el colmillo
dental bridge	el puente dental
denture	la dentadura postiza
front tooth	el incisivo
gum	la encía
molar	la muela
palate	el paladar
tongue	la lengua
tonsils	las amígdalas
tooth	el diente
toothache	el dolor de muela
wisdom tooth	la muela del juicio

Arm and hand

armpit
elbow
finger
fingernail
fist
forearm
index finger
knuckle
muscle
nail
pinkie, little finger
shoulder
thumb
wrist

El brazo y la mano

la axila; el sobaco
el codo
el dedo
la uña
el puño
el antebrazo
el índice
el nudillo
el músculo
la uña
el meñique
el hombro
el pulgar; el dedo gordo
la muñeca

Leg and foot

ankle
bunion
calf
corn
feet
heavy
heel
instep
knee
leg
shin
sole
thigh
toe

La pierna y el pie

el tobillo
el juanete
la pantorrilla
el callo
los pies
pesado, -a
el talón
el empeine
la rodilla
la pierna
la espinilla
la planta del pie
el muslo
el dedo del pie

Senses

bitter
cold
to hear
hearing
hot
to listen
noise
salty
sense
sight
smell (noun)
to smell
soft
sweet
taste (noun)
to taste
touch (noun)
to touch

Los sentidos

amargo
frío
oír
el oído
calor
escuchar
el ruido
salado, -a
el sentido
la vista
el olfato
oler
suave
dulce
el gusto; el sabor
saber
el tacto
tocar

Health

blister
exercise
fit
fitness
good shape: to be in good shape
harmful
healthy
mental health
to prevent
preventive medicine
unhealthy
vigor
vigorous
well-being

Hygiene

bath
to bathe
bathroom tissue, toilet paper
bathtub
body odor
clean (adj.)
to clean
deodorant
electric razor
lather (noun)
to lather
period
razor
sanitary napkin
to shave
shower (noun)
to shower
soap
sponge
sweat
tampon
tissue paper
toiletries
towel
trim (noun)
to trim (one's hair, one's beard)
to wash

Hair and nail hygiene

barbershop
beauty salon
brush
to brush one's hair
comb
to comb one's hair

La salud

la ampolla
el ejercicio
en buena forma física
en buen estado físico
estar en forma
dañino, -a
saludable; sano, -a
la salud mental
prevenir
la medicina preventiva
enfermizo; malsano
el vigor
vigoroso, -a
el bienestar

El aseo, la higiene

el baño
bañarse
el papel higiénico
la bañera
el olor del cuerpo
aseado, -a; limpio, -a
asear, asear(se)
el desodorante
la máquina de afeitar eléctrica
la espuma
jabonar, enjabonar
la menstruación; el período; la regla
la cuchilla de afeitar
la toalla sanitaria
afeitarse
la ducha
ducharse
el jabón
la esponja
el sudor
el tampón
el pañuelo de papel
los artículos de aseo personal
la toalla
la barba
recortar el pelo
lavar

La higiene del cabello y de las uñas

la barbería; la peluquería
la peluquería (de señoras); el salón de belleza
el cepillo
cepillarse
el peine
peinarse

Hair and nail hygiene (cont.)	**La higiene del cabello y de las uñas (cont.)**
to cut one's nails	cortarse las uñas
dandruff	la caspa
to file one's nails	limar(se) las uñas
hairbrush	el cepillo de cabello
haircut	el corte de pelo
hair dryer	el secador de pelo
lice	los piojos
lotion	la crema para la piel; la loción
nail brush	el cepillo de uñas
nail clipper	el cortaúñas
nail file	la lima de uñas
scissors	las tijeras
shampoo	el champú
Oral hygiene	**La higiene bucal**
to brush one's teeth	cepillarse los dientes
electric toothbrush	el cepillo eléctrico
floss (noun)	el hilo dental
to floss	limpiar con el hilo dental
gargle, gargling (noun)	la gárgara
to gargle	hacer gárgaras
mouthwash	el enjuague bucal
toothbrush	el cepillo de dientes
toothpaste	la pasta de dientes
toothpick	el mondadientes; el palillo de dientes

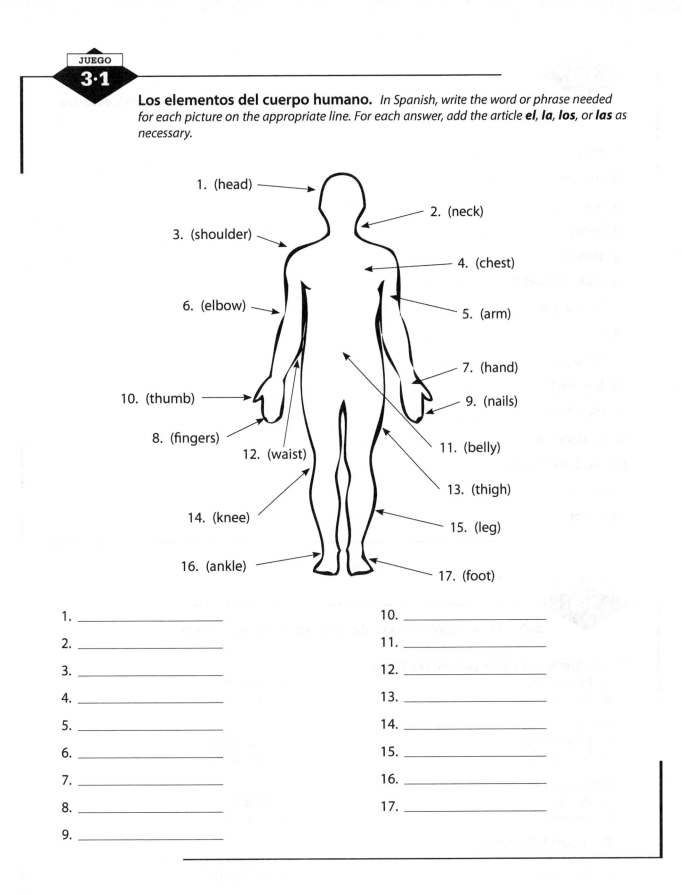

Los elementos del cuerpo humano. *In Spanish, write the word or phrase needed for each picture on the appropriate line. For each answer, add the article **el**, **la**, **los**, or **las** as necessary.*

1. (head)

2. (neck)

3. (shoulder)

4. (chest)

6. (elbow)

5. (arm)

7. (hand)

10. (thumb)

9. (nails)

8. (fingers)

12. (waist)

11. (belly)

13. (thigh)

14. (knee)

15. (leg)

16. (ankle)

17. (foot)

1. _____

2. _____

3. _____

4. _____

5. _____

6. _____

7. _____

8. _____

9. _____

10. _____

11. _____

12. _____

13. _____

14. _____

15. _____

16. _____

17. _____

El cuerpo y la cara. *Translate from English into Spanish and write the article **el**, **la**, **los**, or **las** as necessary.*

1. height __ __ __ __ __ __ __ __
2. muscle __ __ __ __ __ __ __ __ __
3. leg __ __ __ __ __ __ __
4. heavy (f.) __ __ __ __ __ __
5. thin (m.) __ __ __ __ __ __ __
6. dark-skinned (f.) __ __ __ __ __ __
7. freckled (m.) __ __ __ __ __ __
8. scar __ __ __ __ __ __ __ __ __ __
9. mole __ __ __ __ __ __ __
10. bald (m.) __ __ __ __ __
11. blonde (f.) __ __ __ __ __ __
12. straight hair __ __ __ __ __ __ __ __ __ __ __
13. red-haired (m.) __ __ __ __ __ __ __ __ __
14. teeth __ __ __ __ __ __ __ __ __ __
15. molars __ __ __ __ __ __ __ __ __

Selección múltiple. *Choose the best response for each question.*

1. Este hombre no tiene pelo en la cabeza.
   a. Es moreno.
   b. Es rubio.
   c. Es cano.
   d. Es calvo.

2. ¿Te caíste? En tu cara aparece
   a. la piel clara.
   b. la cicatriz.
   c. la espinilla.
   d. la mejilla.

3. En la cara y en la espalda tienes
   a. pecas.
   b. dientes.
   c. labios.
   d. narices.

4. Dentro de la boca hay ...
   a. uñas.
   b. una nuca.
   c. una lengua.
   d. dermatitis.

5. Debajo de cada brazo hay ...
   a. un sobaco.
   b. tres dedos.
   c. un cuello.
   d. dos pestañas.

3·4

Descripciones de la salud y la higiene: Adivinanza. *Guess which word or phrase corresponds to each definition. Write the appropriate article* **el**, **la**, **los**, *or* **las** *as necessary.*

1. La peluquera necesita esto para cortar el pelo. _____

2. Después de cepillarse los dientes por lo general usamos este producto. _____

_____

3. Si nos duele la garganta tenemos que hacer esto. _____

4. No puedo cortar el pelo, por eso siempre voy a este lugar. _____

_____

5. Una chica que corta la uñas. _____

6. Es fácil usar esto para afeitarse en casa. _____

7. Voy a relajarme unos minutos y por eso no voy a usar la ducha sino ésta. _____

_____

8. Muchas personas hacen muchos ejercicios, tienen músculos en los brazos y no tienen barriga: están ... _____

9. Esta familia no padece de Alzheimer ni demencia: disfruta de eso. _____

_____

10. Dejar de fumar y comer frutas, vegetales y pescado es excelente para evitar problemas y forma parte de esto. _____

11. Algunas personas tienen mal olor en el sobaco y es porque no usan este producto. _____

_____

12. Estornudo tanto cuando tengo alergias en casa y uso este producto. _____

_____

3·5

El cuerpo humano: Adivinanza. *Guess which word or phrase corresponds to each definition.*

1. El órgano que impulsa la sangre _____

2. El órgano donde se deposita la orina _____

3. El tamaño de las personas _____

4. Cuando una persona nace, se corta y se seca _____

5. Es necesario comer alimentos con calcio para proteger estos. _____

6. Entre la mano y el brazo _____

7. Pelo del cuerpo pero no el de la cabeza _____

8. Entre el pie y la rodilla _____

9. El dedo más gordo de la mano _____

10. Entre la clavícula y el brazo _____

11. El dedo de la mano para indicar o mostrar alguna cosa _____

12. La mano cerrada _____

13. Entre el antebrazo y el hombro _____

14. Todos los huesos que contiene el cuerpo _____

15. El órgano que cubre todo el cuerpo _____

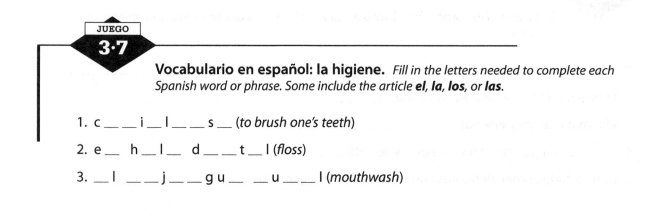

JUEGO 3·6

Un juego de palabras. *For each category below, choose the word or phrase that does* ***not*** *belong.*

1. **los productos para la higiene** el desodorante, la basura, el papel higiénico, el jabón

2. **la mala salud** dañino, enfermizo, malsano, sano

3. **los sentidos** el talón, el olor, el sonido, el gusto

4. **las partes de la cabeza** el cabello, la nariz, el pecho, la boca

5. **la descripción del pelo** rizado, regordete, canoso, lacio

6. **las partes de la boca** el labio, la lengua, el diente, la pantorrilla

7. **los dientes** la muela, el colmillo, el incisivo, la amígdala

8. **las partes del ojo** la mandíbula, la pestaña, el párpado, la pupila

9. **la apariencia en la cara** la patilla, el bigote, la barba, el dedo

10. **las partes de los pies** el talón, el dedo, la pantorrilla, la planta

JUEGO 3·7

Vocabulario en español: la higiene. *Fill in the letters needed to complete each Spanish word or phrase. Some include the article* ***el***, ***la***, ***los***, *or* ***las***.

1. c __ __ i __ l __ __ s __ (*to brush one's teeth*)

2. e __ h __ l __ d __ __ t __ l (*floss*)

3. __ l __ __ j __ __ g u __ __ u __ __ l (*mouthwash*)

4. j __ __ o __ a __ s __ (*to lather*)

5. l __ m __ __ __ __ t r __ a __ __ ó __ (*period*)

6. __ l m __ __ d __ __ i __ __ t __s (*toothpick*)

7. e __ c __ r t __ __ e __ __ l __ (*haircut*)

8. __ a l __ __ __ __ d __ __ ñ __ s (*nail file*)

9. __ __ p e __ __ e (*comb*)

10. l __ c __ __ p __ (*dandruff*)

11. l __ t __ __ l l __ (*towel*)

12. __ a v __ __ __ (*to wash*)

13. e __ o __ __ r __ e __ c __ __ r __ o (*body odor*)

14. l __ e __ p u __ __ (*lather*)

15. m __ __ s __ n __ (*unhealthy*)

JUEGO

3·8

Palabras aprendidas. *Translate these words from English into Spanish. (Don't forget the article **el** or **la** as needed.) Reading down the boxed column will then reveal a Spanish word or phrase.*

1. nose (*f.*) ▦ __   __ __ __ __ __ __

2. nape (*f.*) __ __   __ __ __ ▦

3. sideburn (*f.*) __ __ ▦ __ __ __ __ __ __

4. neck (*m.*) __ __   __ ▦ __ __ __ __

5. eyelash (*f.*) __ __   __ ▦ __ __ __ __ __

6. scar (*f.*) __ __   __ __ __ __ __ __ ▦ __

7. skin (*f.*) __ __   __ __ __ ▦

8. eyebrow (*f.*) __ ▦   __ __ __ __ __

9. palate (*m.*) __ __   __ __ __ __ __ ▦ __ __

10. gum (*f.*) __ __   ▦ __ __ __ __

11. tongue (*f.*) __ __   ▦ __ __ __ __ __

12. canine tooth (*m.*) __ __   __ ▦ __ __ __ __ __

13. cheek (*f.*) __ __   __ __ ▦ __ __ __ __

14. ear (*f.*) __ __   __ ▦ __ __ __ __

La palabra vertical: _____

Un juego acróstico. *Translate the clues on the left from English into Spanish. (You do not need to add articles.) Reading down the first letter of each word will then reveal a Spanish word.*

1. to wash ▨ __ __ __ __
2. hygiene (*m.*) ▨ __ __ __
3. liver (*m.*) ▨ __ __ __ __ __
4. intestine (*m.*) ▨ __ __ __ __ __ __ __
5. gargle (*f.*) ▨ __ __ __ __ __ __
6. front tooth (*m.*) ▨ __ __ __ __ __ __ __
7. gum (*f.*) ▨ __ __ __ __
8. knuckle (*m.*) ▨ __ __ __ __ __
9. instep (*m.*) ▨ __ __ __ __ __ __
10. beard (*f.*) ▨ __ __ __ __
11. nails (*f.*) ▨ __ __ __
12. lotion (*f.*) ▨ __ __ __ __
13. blister (*f.*) ▨ __ __ __ __ __ __
14. mole (*m.*) ▨ __ __ __ __

La palabra vertical: _____

Juego de respuestas y preguntas. *Write a question for every answer given below.*

Los sentidos

1. Escuchamos. _____
2. Vemos. _____
3. Huele muy sabroso. _____
4. Es muy suave, no es duro. _____

La salud

5. Una comida que no es dañina. _____
6. Una persona que hace muchos ejercicios todos los días. _____
7. Una chica que sufre de catarros varias veces al año. _____
8. Un problema que uno tiene debajo del pie y que uno no puede bien caminar._____
   _____

El aseo

9. Algo en el cabello que produce que uno no puede ir a clase. _____

10. Algo que uno tiene que usar cuando las uñas de los pies son demasiadas largas. _____

_____

11. Un producto que usamos para lavarnos bien el pelo. _____

_____

12. Un producto que usamos cuando tenemos la piel seca. _____

_____

Palabras revueltas o anagrama de este capítulo. *Unscramble each Spanish word below and write it out correctly.*

El cuerpo

1. r / e / o / b / c / r / e _____

2. á / d / o / p / r / a / p _____

3. e / r / t / n / f / e _____

4. p / c / e / a _____

5. a / s / c / o / a / n _____

6. s / e / r / t / o / r / a / _____

7. ó / c / z / n / a / r / o _____

La salud

8. a / u / l / s / l / e / b / a / d _____

9. r / p / e / n / e / v / i / r _____

10. c / i / e / j / i / r / c / e / o _____

11. o / s / e / d / a / o / t / n / e / r / d _____

La higiene

12. j / e / p / a / s / o / n _____

13. ó / n / l / i / c / o _____

14. r / e / a / i / j / t / s _____

15. s / i / o / j / p / o _____

Palabras escondidas en este juego de puzle. *Find and circle the Spanish words hidden vertically, horizontally, and diagonally.*

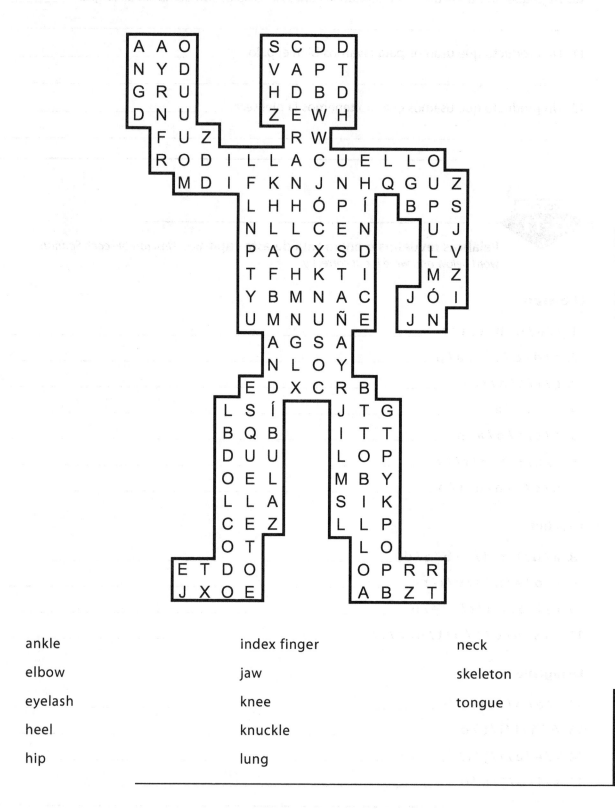

ankle	index finger	neck
elbow	jaw	skeleton
eyelash	knee	tongue
heel	knuckle	
hip	lung	

Crucigrama. *Fill in the crossword puzzle with the Spanish words.*

Horizontales (*Across*)

1. vigorous (*f.*)
7. shampoo
10. toothpick
12. to shave
13. skeleton
15. scar
16. healthy
18. wrinkle
20. gargle
21. scissors
22. waist

Verticales (*Down*)

2. sense
3. to bathe
4. dandruff
5. lotion
6. slender (*f.*)
8. beauty salon
9. well-being
10. muscular (*f.*)
11. towel
14. lather
17. mustache
19. plump (*m.*)

Las enfermedades y el cuidado médico

Illnesses and medical care

Las etapas de la vida

Stages of life

Illnesses and medical conditions / **Las enfermedades y los sufrimientos**

Illnesses and medical conditions	Las enfermedades y los sufrimientos
to become ill	enfermar, enfermarse
blind person	el ciego, la ciega; el/la invidente
breathless	sin aliento
corn (on foot)	el callo
deaf	mudo, -a
deafness	la sordera
dementia	la demencia
disability	la discapacidad; la incapacidad
discomfort	el malestar; el trastorno
dizzy	mareado, -a
dizzy spell	el mareo
to feel	sentirse
to get better	mejorar, mejorarse
handicapped	discapacitado, -a
hospital	el hospital
to hurt	doler
ill	enfermo, -a
illness	la enfermedad; la dolencia
pain	el dolor
paralysis	la parálisis
patient	el enfermo, la enferma; el/la paciente
pimple	el grano
rheumatism	el reuma; el reumatismo
sick	enfermo, -a
so-so	regular
to suffer	sufrir
suffering	el sufrimiento
trauma	el trauma
unconscious	inconsciente
under the weather	indispuesto, -a
weak	débil
well	bien
to worsen, to get worse	empeorar, empeorarse

40

Colds and gastrointestinal ailments

chill (noun)	el escalofrío
cold	el catarro; el resfriado
cough (noun)	la tos
to cough	toser
diarrhea	la diarrea
earache	el dolor de oído
fever	la fiebre
flu	la gripa; la gripe
to have a cold	tener catarro; tener resfriado
infection	la infección
migraine	la migraña
upset stomach	el trastorno estomacal
vomit (noun)	el vómito
to vomit	vomitar

Chronic disorders

allergy	la alergia
appendicitis	la apendicitis
arthritis	la artritis
asthma	el asma
to bleed	sangrar
to bleed to death	desangrarse
blood	la sangre
blood pressure	la presión arterial
bronchitis	la bronquitis
cancer	el cáncer
cut (noun)	la cortada
diabetes	la diabetes
emergency	la urgencia
heart attack	el infarto; el ataque al corazón
heart disease	las enfermedades del corazón
high blood pressure	la hipertensión
injured person	el herido, la herida
injury	la herida
pacemaker	el marcapaso
pneumonia	la neumonía; la pulmonía
swelling	la hinchazón; la inflamación
swollen	inflamado, -a; hinchado, -a
syringe	la jeringuilla
tonsillitis	la amigdalitis
tuberculosis	la tuberculosis

Medical care

anesthetic	la anestesia; el anestésico
anesthetist	el/la anestesista
blanket	la manta
blood test	el análisis de sangre
cast	la escayola
clinic	la clínica
condition	el estado

Los resfriados y los sufrimientos gastrointestinales

Los sufrimientos crónicos

El cuidado médico

Medical care (cont.) El cuidado médico (cont.)

critical condition	el estado grave
doctor	el médico, la médica; el doctor, la doctora
doctor's office	el consultorio
dressing	el vendaje; la venda
emergency room	la sala de urgencias
first aid	los primeros auxilios
fracture	la fractura
fractured arm	el brazo fracturado
gynecologist	el ginecólogo, la ginecóloga
intensive care unit (ICU)	la unidad de cuidados intensivos (UCI)
medical exam	el reconocimiento médico
medical insurance	el seguro médico
nurse	el enfermero, la enfermera
office hours	las horas de oficina
operating room	el quirófano
operation	la operación
outpatient clinic	el ambulatorio
recovery room	la sala de recuperación
rest (noun)	el descanso; el reposo
to rest	descansar; reposar
to resuscitate	reanimar
robotic surgery	la cirugía robótica
surgeon	el cirujano, la cirujana
surgery	la cirugía
surgical	quirúrgico, -a
syringe	la jeringuilla
therapist	el/la terapeuta
thermometer	el termómetro
treatment	el tratamiento
vitamin	la vitamina
wheelchair	la silla de ruedas

Medications Los medicamentos

analgesic	el analgésico
antibiotic	el antibiótico
bandage	el esparadrapo; la venda
Band-Aid	la bandita; la tirita
birth control pill	la píldora anticonceptiva
cough medicine	el jarabe (para la tos)
cure (noun)	la cura
to cure	curar
drops	las gotas
drug	la medicina
eyedropper	el cuentagotas; el gotero
first-aid kit	la caja de primeros auxilios
injection, shot	la inyección
medicine	el medicamento; la medicina
ointment	la pomada
pharmacist	el farmacéutico, la farmacéutica
pill, tablet	la píldora; la tableta
prescription	la receta médica
therapy	la terapia

Dental care

abscess	el absceso; el flemón
cavity	la caries
dentist	el/la dentista; el odontólogo, la odontóloga
filling	el empaste
fluoride	el flúor
orthodontics	la ortodoncia
plaque	la placa
to pull a tooth	sacar un diente
toothache	el dolor de muela

El cuidado dental

Eye care

cataract	la catarata
contact lens	la lentilla de contacto
eye doctor	el/la oculista
eyeglasses	las gafas; los lentes; los espejuelos
optician	el óptico
to see	ver
sight	la vista

El cuidado de la vista

Psychological conditions and addictions

alcohol	la bebida alcohólica
alcoholic (noun)	el alcohólico, la alcohólica
alcoholism	el alcoholismo
anorexia	la anorexia
bulimia	la bulimia
cocaine	la cocaína; la coca
depressed	deprimido, -a
depression	la depresión
drug	la droga; el estupefaciente
drug addiction	la drogadicción
insane	loco, -a
marijuana	la mariguana
neurosis	la neurosis
nicotine poisoning	el tabaquismo
to smoke	fumar
stress	el estrés

Las condiciones sicológicas y las adicciones

Stages of life

adulthood	la adultez
agony	la agonía
to bear (a child), to give birth	parir; dar luz
birth	el nacimiento
birth certificate	el certificado; la partida de nacimiento
birthday	el cumpleaños
born: to be born	nacer
childhood	la niñez
to die	morir
to live	vivir
middle age	la madurez

Las etapas de la vida

Stages of life (cont.)

old	viejo, -a
old age	la vejez
pension	la pensión; el retiro
people	la gente; las personas
retirement	la jubilación; el retiro
social security	la seguridad social
young	joven
youth	la juventud

Death   La muerte

afterlife	la otra vida; el más allá
ashes	las cenizas
body	el cuerpo; el cadáver; el difunto, la difunta
burial	el entierro
to bury	enterrar
cemetery	el cementerio
condolence(s)	el pésame
cremation	la cremación
death certificate	el certificado de defunción
epitaph	el epitafio
funeral	el funeral
funeral home	la funeraria
heir	el heredero, la heredera
to inherit	heredar
inheritance	la herencia
to live	vivir
mourning	el luto
to pass away	fallecer
remains	los restos mortales
RIP, rest in peace	DEP, descanse en paz
tomb	la tumba
tombstone	la lápida
wake	el velorio
will	el testamento

Cognados. *Translate these words from English into Spanish; include the article **el** or **la** as appropriate.*

1. diabetes (*f.*) _____

2. arthritis (*f.*) _____

3. asthma (*m.*) _____

4. dementia (*f.*) _____

5. vitamin (*f.*) _____

6. injection (*f.*) _____

7. bronchitis (*f.*) _____

8. alcoholism (*m.*) _____

9. doctor (*m./f.*) _____

10. marijuana (*f.*) _____

11. anorexia (*f.*) _____

12. bulimia (*f.*) _____

13. rheumatism (*m.*) _____

14. cocaine (*f.*) _____

15. neurosis (*f.*) _____

16. hospital (*m.*) _____

17. laxative (*m.*) _____

18. operation (*f.*) _____

19. addiction (*f.*) _____

20. stress (*m.*) _____

Palabras aprendidas. *Words you've learned in this and earlier chapters: translate these words from English into Spanish and include the articles **el**, **la**, **los**, and **las** as necessary.*

1. brain _____

2. bone _____

3. ear _____

4. emergency _____

5. toothache _____

6. molar _____

7. doctor's office _____

8. arm _____

9. heart _____

10. leg _____

11. pharmacy _____

12. tonsils _____

13. eyeglasses _____

14. tongue _____

15. body _____

16. intestine _____

Sinónimos. *Write the letter that corresponds to the synonym of each word on the appropriate numbered line.*

1. _____ el retiro	a. la doctora
2. _____ la píldora	b. la hinchazón
3. _____ el dentista	c. la incapacidad
4. _____ la médica	d. la tableta
5. _____ el descanso	e. la medicina
6. _____ el medicamento	f. el analgésico
7. _____ la tirita	g. la pensión
8. _____ la venda	h. el odontólogo
9. _____ el catarro	i. el vendaje
10. _____ la discapacidad	j. el reposo
11. _____ la neumonía	k. el invidente
12. _____ la inflamación	l. la bandita
13. _____ la ciego	m. la pulmonía
14. _____ la analgesia	n. el resfriado

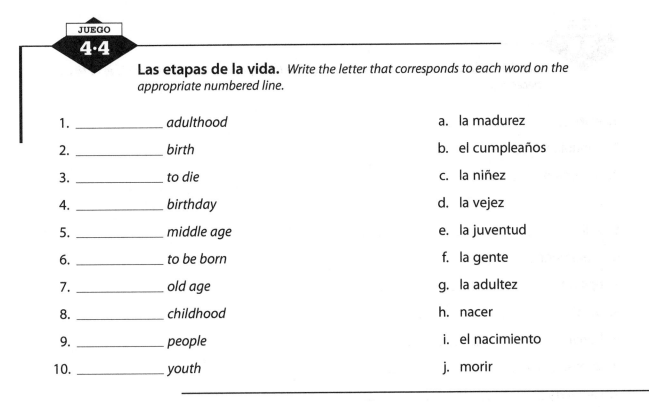

JUEGO 4·4

Las etapas de la vida. *Write the letter that corresponds to each word on the appropriate numbered line.*

1. _____ adulthood
2. _____ birth
3. _____ to die
4. _____ birthday
5. _____ middle age
6. _____ to be born
7. _____ old age
8. _____ childhood
9. _____ people
10. _____ youth

a. la madurez
b. el cumpleaños
c. la niñez
d. la vejez
e. la juventud
f. la gente
g. la adultez
h. nacer
i. el nacimiento
j. morir

JUEGO 4·5

Selección múltiple. *Choose the best response for each question.*

1. Esta persona fuma mucho y padece de ...
   a. el alcoholismo.
   b. la parálisis.
   c. la anestesia.
   d. el tabaquismo.

2. Lola usa el lenguaje de señas (*sign language*) porque padece de ...
   a. la sordera.
   b. la hipertensión.
   c. la diabetes.
   d. la parálisis.

3. Esta palabra es un sinónimo de la droga.
   a. el cáncer
   b. la herida
   c. la depresión
   d. el estupefaciente

4. Dentro de la boca tienes dolor porque padeces de ...
   a. neumonía.
   b. diabetes.
   c. amigdalitis.
   d. dermatitis.

5. Me duele la cabeza y voy a tomar ...
   a. un analgésico.
   b. un jarabe para la tos.
   c. un antibiótico.
   d. un termómetro.

Las enfermedades y el cuidado médico • Las etapas de la vida   47

La vida y la muerte. *Translate from English into Spanish; include the article **el** or **la** as necessary.*

1. wake __ __   __ __ __ __ __ __ __

2. condolence __ __   __ __ __ __ __ __ __

3. mourning __ __   __ __ __ __ __

4. life __ __   __ __ __ __ __

5. will __ __   __ __ __ __ __ __ __ __ __ __

6. retirement __ __   __ __ __ __ __ __ __ __ __ __ __

7. epitaph __ __   __ __ __ __ __ __ __ __

8. death __ __   __ __ __ __ __ __ __

9. burial __ __   __ __ __ __ __ __ __ __ __

10. to pass away __ __ __ __ __ __ __ __ __ __

11. cemetery __ __   __ __ __ __ __ __ __ __ __ __ __

12. heir (*f.*) __ __   __ __ __ __ __ __ __ __ __ __

13. to live __ __ __ __ __ __

14. agony __ __   __ __ __ __ __ __ __ __

15. cremation __ __   __ __ __ __ __ __ __ __ __ __ __ __

La salud. ¿Verdadero o falso? *Indicate whether each statement below is true (**V**) or false (**F**).*

1. _____ Me duele el pie porque tengo dos callos.

2. _____ Cuando tengo una cortada me pongo una bandita.

3. _____ Tomo el antibiótico para mejorar el reumatismo.

4. _____ Posiblemente la joven lleva una escayola porque tiene dolor de oídos.

5. _____ Puedo pagar a mi doctora y al hospital porque tengo el seguro médico.

6. _____ Si tienes un dolor de cabeza debes ir a la unidad de cuidados intensivos.

7. _____ Cuando tienes fiebre, puedes usar el marcapaso.

8. _____ Si siento un dolor muy grande en mi pecho, puedo ir al hospital para mi salud.

9. _____ La diabetes es igual que el asma.

10. _____ El anestésico evita el dolor durante la operación quirúrgica.

11. _____ La píldora anticonceptiva ayuda a bajar la fiebre.

12. _____ Si tengo dolor de muelas voy al ginecólogo.

JUEGO
4·8

Palabras escondidas en este juego de puzle. *Find and circle the Spanish equivalents of these words hidden vertically, horizontally, and diagonally.*

```
X  E  I  P  Z  B  D  S  O  V  L  O  O  A  K
M  A  R  E  O  E  O  C  R  H  Z  N  Z  R  B
W  Q  A  I  J  T  L  Q  L  N  A  R  A  C  N
E  H  L  A  D  U  O  E  X  R  E  R  A  A  Q
M  T  Q  V  L  S  R  T  G  C  O  L  N  L  D
P  R  S  P  Z  N  M  M  N  J  Y  S  R  L  O
E  S  S  A  S  X  U  Á  E  Z  H  H  T  O  L
O  B  J  K  N  D  C  M  H  X  U  A  I  C  E
R  O  P  B  Q  G  V  P  M  E  A  E  F  D  R
A  Y  K  R  V  Y  R  F  I  E  B  R  E  C  P
R  M  W  N  E  W  F  A  B  Y  L  B  I  E  J
I  A  H  K  Q  K  O  Q  R  O  S  Q  D  F  R
S  N  S  U  F  R  I  R  H  Q  X  H  C  A  G
Q  T  K  K  S  N  Y  D  V  Ó  M  I  T  O  B
H  A  T  E  L  R  F  P  W  G  M  T  R  O  E
```

blanket	dizzy spell	pimple
to bleed	fever	to suffer
cancer	to get better	vomit (*noun*)
corn	to hurt	to worsen
cough	pain	

Un juego acróstico. *Translate these words from English into Spanish. (You do not need to include the articles.) Reading down the first letter of each word will then reveal a Spanish word, with its article.*

1. contact lenses ▨ __ __ __ __ __ __ __ __

2. adulthood ▨ __ __ __ __ __ __

3. birthday ▨ __ __ __ __ __ __ __ __ __

4. asthma ▨ __ __ __

5. upset stomach ▨ __ __ __ __ __ __ __ __ __ __ __ __ __ __ __ __

6. appendicitis ▨ __ __ __ __ __ __ __ __ __

7. resuscitate ▨ __ __ __ __ __ __ __

8. antibiotic ▨ __ __ __ __ __ __ __ __ __

9. therapist ▨ __ __ __ __ __ __ __

10. anorexia ▨ __ __ __ __ __ __ __

La palabra vertical: _____

Crucigrama. *Fill in the crossword puzzle with the Spanish words.*

Horizontales (*Across*)

1. funeral
3. ointment
7. to bury

8. abscess
10. ashes
11. infection

14. migraine
15. to die
16. to give birth

Verticales (*Down*)

2. pension
4. illness
5. inheritance

6. plaque
9. stage
12. fluoride

13. childhood
14. drug

¡La urgencia! Los primeros auxilios y los tratamientos: palabras escondidas en este juego de puzle. *Find and circle the Spanish equivalents of these words hidden vertically, horizontally, and diagonally.*

```
            D I A R R F H
            P É C O P G W
            R H B X Q P A
            E W E I L N Z
            S G Y U L E H
            I N F A R T O
I Z J I H X Ó T E R M Ó M E T R O A X
U U H J K N N O T V A S X A J O L E W
P R E E S C A Y O L A C D U Z L S S R
L S G N A T R A U M A A T N I O G T X
S E J E F C T P L L E N I U T E M A P
K O D T N E E C E R Y S G N R T F D A
L G P J L C R L A O A N E M Y A G O I
            I M M T I I K
            A A O R L U C
            L G E A R A O
            H J N V B Y H
            C I R U G Í A
            S H Q I R C H
```

blood pressure (*2 words*)	heart attack
breathless (*2 words*)	patient (*m.*)
cast	surgery
condition	syringe
dizzy (*f.*)	thermometer
drops	trauma
emergency	weak
fracture	

La casa y el domicilio

House and home

Housing and surroundings | Las viviendas y los alredededores

Housing and surroundings	Las viviendas y los alredededores
amenities	las comodidades en casa
apartment, flat	el apartamento
apartment house	el edificio de apartamentos
building	el edificio
city block	la manzana
condominium	el condominio
first floor	la planta baja
floor	el piso
home	el domicilio
house	la casa
housing	la vivienda
neighborhood	el barrio
park	el parque
residential area	la urbanización
street	la calle
view	la vista

Home features | Las características de la casa

Home features	Las características de la casa
air conditioning	el aire acondicionado
alarm	la alarma
awning	el toldo
balcony	el balcón
basement	el sótano
cable	el cable eléctrico
door	la puerta
downstairs	abajo
entrance	la entrada
exit	la salida
façade	la fachada
fan	el ventilador
fireplace	la chimenea
furniture	el mueble, los muebles
garage	el garaje
hallway	el pasillo
heating	la calefacción
key	la llave
lock (noun)	la cerradura
to lock	cerrar con llave
patio	el patio

Home features (cont.)

railing	la barandilla
roof	el techo
room	el cuarto
security	la seguridad
socket	el enchufe
stairs	la escalera
terrace	la terraza
to turn off the light	apagar la luz
to turn on the light	encender la luz
upstairs	arriba
wall	la pared
window	la ventana
windowpane	el vidrio de la ventana

Renting, selling, and buying

agency	la agencia
agent	el/la agente
to borrow	pedir dinero prestado
to buy	comprar
deposit (noun)	el depósito
to deposit	depositar
lease	el contrato
loan (noun)	el préstamo
to loan	prestar
money	el dinero
mortgage (noun)	la hipoteca
to mortgage	hipotecar
move (noun)	la mudanza
to move	mudarse
owner	el dueño, la dueña
real estate agency	la inmobiliaria
rent (noun)	el alquiler
to rent	alquilar
to sell	vender
shopping	la compra
title deed	el documento de propiedad

Repairs, remodeling, and tools

brush	la brocha
hammer (noun)	el martillo
to hammer	martillar
to install	instalar
to lay a floor	instalar un piso
nail (noun)	la puntilla
paint (noun)	la pintura
to paint	pintar
to remove	sacar
repair (noun)	la reparación
to repair	reparar
saw (noun)	el serrucho
to saw	serruchar
screw	el tornillo

Las características de la casa (cont.)

Alquilar, vender y comprar

Las reparaciones, remodelar y los utensilios

Repairs, remodeling, and tools (cont.)

screwdriver	desatornillar; el destornillador
tool	el utensilio, la herramienta
wallpaper (noun)	el papel para empapelar las paredes
to wallpaper	empapelar
wallpaper glue	el pegamento

Rooms: elements in each room

Bathroom

air freshener	el ambientador
bathroom sink	el lavabo
bathtub	la bañera
bidet	el bidé
faucet	la llave del agua
hair dryer	la secadora de pelo
medicine cabinet	el botiquín para medicinas
mirror	el espejo
shower	la ducha
soap dish	la jabonera
toilet	el inodoro
toilet paper	el papel higiénico
towel	la toalla
towel rack	el toallero

Bedroom

alarm clock	el despertador
bed	la cama
bedroom	el dormitorio, el cuarto para dormir
blanket	la manta
bunk bed	la litera
closet	el clóset
curtain	la cortina
drawer	el cajón
hanger	el perchero
mattress	el colchón
night table	la mesita de noche
pillow	la almohada
pillowcase	la funda
sheet	la sábana
wardrobe	el armario

Dining room

bottle opener	el abrebotellas
chair	la silla
cup	la taza
dining table	la mesa de comedor
dish	el plato
fork	el tenedor
glass	el vaso
knife	el cuchillo
napkin	la servilleta
place setting	el cubierto; los cubiertos

Las reparaciones, remodelar y los utensilios (cont.)

Las habitaciones: elementos en cada habitación

El baño

El dormitorio

El comedor

Dining room (cont.)	El comedor (cont.)
sideboard	el aparador
spoon	la cuchara
sugar bowl	el azucarero
table	la mesa
tablecloth	el mantel
teapot	la tetera
teaspoon	la cucharita
tray	la bandeja
wine	el vino
wineglass	la copa de vino

Kitchen and electric appliances	La cocina y los electrodomésticos
apron	el delantal
coffee maker	la cafetera
container	el recipiente
to cook	cocinar
countertop	la encimera
dishwasher	el lavaplatos
drawer	el cajón
electric can opener	el abrelatas eléctrico
electric skillet	el sartén eléctrico
electric stove	la cocina eléctrica
faucet	la llave de agua
freezer	el congelador
frying pan	el sartén
garbage disposal	el triturador de basura
gas stove	la cocina de gas
kitchen sink	el fregadero
microwave oven	el microondas
oven	el horno
paper towel	la toalla de papel
pot	la olla
refrigerator	el refrigerador
stool	el taburete
trash can	el contenedor de basura
water faucet	el grifo de cocina

Living room	La sala, el salón
armchair	el sillón
bench	el banco
bookshelf	el librero
cable TV	la televisión por cable
coffee table	la mesa de centro
digital TV	la televisión digital
hearth	el hogar
lamp	la lámpara
sofa	el sofá
TV	la tele; la televisión
vase	el florero

Chores and utensils	Los quehaceres y los utensilios
broom	la escoba
brush	el cepillo
to clean	limpiar
cleaner	el limpiador
to clear the table	quitar la mesa
clothes laundry basket	el cesto de la ropa (sucia)
to do laundry	lavar la ropa
to do the dishes	fregar los platos
to drain	escurrir los platos
to dry	secar
dryer	la secadora de ropa
to dust	sacudir el polvo
to fix	arreglar
garbage, trash	la basura
housework	los quehaceres
iron (noun)	la plancha
to iron	planchar
to iron, press clothes	planchar (la ropa)
laundry room	el cuarto para guardar y lavar la ropa
to make the bed	hacer la cama
to mop	fregar el piso
to put in order	ordenar
to sweep	barrer
to take out the trash	sacar la basura
to tidy up	arreglar
to vacuum	pasar la aspiradora
vacuum cleaner	la aspiradora
to wash	fregar; lavar
washing machine	la lavadora

Food preparation	La preparación de los alimentos
barbecue	la barbacoa
to boil	hervir
breakfast (noun)	el desayuno
to breakfast	desayunar
to broil	asar
to dine	cenar
dinner	la cena
to fry	freír
to have breakfast	desayunar
lunch (noun)	el almuerzo
to lunch	almorzar

Cognados. *Translate these words from English into Spanish; include the article **el** or **la** as necessary.*

1. digital TV _____

2. refrigerator _____

3. terrace _____

4. electric _____

5. apartment _____

6. park _____

7. patio _____

8. agent _____

9. curtain _____

10. closet _____

11. to repair _____

12. barbecue _____

13. air conditioning _____

14. condominium _____

15. sofa _____

16. bidet _____

17. agency _____

18. deposit _____

19. oven _____

20. freezer _____

La vivienda y los alrededores. *Translate from English into Spanish. (You do not need to include articles.)*

1. block __ __ __ __ __ __

2. hallway __ __ __ __ __ __ __

3. security __ __ __ __ __ __ __ __ __

4. street __ __ __ __ __

5. residential area __ __ __ __ __ __ __ __ __ __ __ __

6. neighborhood __ __ __ __ __ __

7. housing __ __ __ __ __ __ __

8. apartment __ __ __ __ __ __ __ __ __

9. building __ __ __ __ __ __ __

10. hearth __ __ __ __ __

Selección múltiple. *Choose the best response for each question.*

1. Elena vive en el tercer piso.
   a. Trabaja en el techo.
   b. Usa la escalera.
   c. Sube por la barandilla.
   d. Apaga la luz.

2. Tenemos mucho calor en casa.
   a. Encendemos muchas luces.
   b. Cerramos las puertas.
   c. Abrimos las ventanas.
   d. Rompemos el vidrio de la terraza.

3. No puedes abrir la puerta de tu casa porque tú no tienes ...
   a. la cerradura.
   b. la silla
   c. la entrada al techo.
   d. la llave.

4. Lisa puede ver este canal de televisión de Inglaterra porque ...
   a. tiene el cable para la televisión.
   b. usa la mesa de centro.
   c. usa el aire acondicionado.
   d. conecta la tele con el ventilador.

5. Lo opuesto de encender es ...
   a. abrir.
   b. interrumpir.
   c. apagar.
   d. alambrar.

Un juego de palabras. *For each category below, choose the word or phrase that does not belong.*

1. **los usos para preparar las comidas** hervir, asar, barrer, freír

2. **los quehaceres en casa** negar, fregar, lavar, planchar

3. **los muebles en casa** el taburete, la almohada, el banco, el sillón

4. **los elementos de la cocina** la cafetera, el vaso, el sartén eléctrico, la hipoteca

5. **los documentos para tener un apartamento** el depósito, la hipoteca, el papel higiénico, el préstamo

6. **las reparaciones en casa** reparar el techo, pintar las paredes, instalar el piso, lavar las ropas

7. **las necesidades en algunos espacios en casa** el ambientador, el botiquín de medicinas, el domicilio, la chimenea

8. **las herramientas en casa** el serrucho, la furgoneta, la llave, los martillos

9. **el dormitorio** el colchón, la sábana, el despertador, la llave de agua

10. **las necesidades para limpiar en casa** la aspiradora, el cepillo, la lámpara, el limpiador

Palabras revueltas. *Unscramble these words and write the Spanish word. The first word is done for you.*

1. o / a / n / t / ó / s (*m.*) <u>sótano</u>

2. l / a / u / q / i / e / r / l (*m.*) _____

3. l / o / t / o / d (*m.*) _____

4. p / a / n / l / h / a / c (*f.*) _____

5. h / e / i / a / c / m / e / n (*f.*) _____

6. c / e / o / t / h (*m.*) _____

7. r / t / u / r / a / t / d / i / r / o (*m.*) _____

8. a / d / i / s / l / a (*f.*) _____

9. r / f / e / g / d / a / r / e / o (*m.*) _____

10. i / v / e / i / v / d / n / a (f.) _____

11. l / e / r / o / b / r / i (m.) _____

12. a / g / r / e / a / j (m.) _____

13. d / u / r / a / r / c / e / r / a (f.) _____

14. c / ó / c / a / f / c / a / i / n / l / e (f.) _____

15. i / m / r / c / o / o / d / n / a / s (m.) _____

Adivinanza: ¿de qué habitación, lugar de la casa, objeto o utensilio se trata? *Guess which word or phrase corresponds to each definition.*

1. La ducha para lavarse el pelo y el cuerpo está aquí. _____

2. Esto se coloca sobre la cama. _____

3. La lavadora y la secadora de ropas están aquí. _____

4. Esto es para entrar a la casa. _____

5. El aparador con los platos está aquí. _____

6. El abrelatas eléctrico y el sartén eléctrico están aquí. _____

7. El hogar para calentar el lugar está aquí. _____

8. Esto es para poner la lámpara al lado de la cama. _____

9. La litera es para que dos niños puedan dormir fácilmente en esta habitación. _____

_____

10. Aquí están el toallero y las toallas. _____

11. Esto es para tomar el sol. _____

12. Esto es para ir de un dormitorio a otro. _____

13. Esto se usa para colocar el té. _____

14. Esto se usa para poner el azúcar. _____

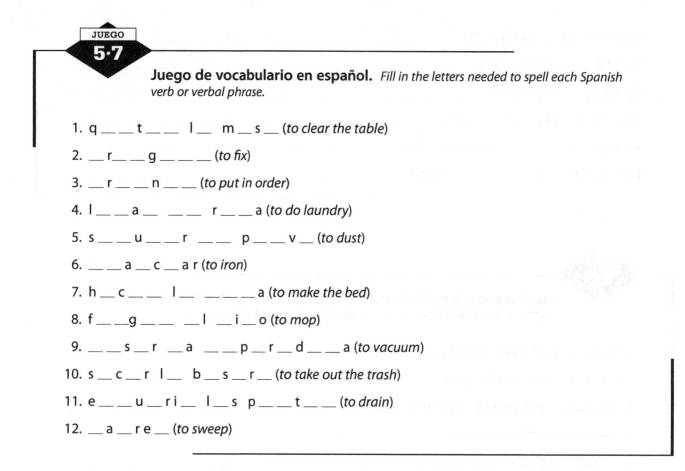

JUEGO 5·7

Juego de vocabulario en español. *Fill in the letters needed to spell each Spanish verb or verbal phrase.*

1. q __ __ t __ __ l __ m __ s __ (*to clear the table*)

2. __ r __ g __ __ __ (*to fix*)

3. __ r __ __ n __ __ (*to put in order*)

4. l __ __ a __ __ __ r __ __ a (*to do laundry*)

5. s __ __ u __ __ r __ __ p __ __ v __ (*to dust*)

6. __ __ a __ c __ a r (*to iron*)

7. h __ c __ __ l __ __ __ __ a (*to make the bed*)

8. f __ __ g __ __ __ l __ i __ o (*to mop*)

9. __ __ s __ r __ a __ __ p __ r __ d __ __ a (*to vacuum*)

10. s __ c __ r l __ b __ s __ r __ (*to take out the trash*)

11. e __ __ u __ r i __ l __ s p __ __ t __ __ (*to drain*)

12. __ a __ r e __ (*to sweep*)

JUEGO 5·8

Juego de respuestas y preguntas. *Write a question for every answer given below.*

La vivienda

1. Vemos por la ventana la playa y la piscina. _____

2. Para pasar de un dormitorio a otro dormitorio. _____

3. Un lugar debajo de la casa en caso de tornado. _____

4. En tu casa tienes lugares para guardar dos autos. _____

Vender y comprar

5. Un lugar de trabajo para vender y comprar casas y apartamentos. _____

_____

6. Una persona que tiene muchas propiedades. _____

7. Pagar el dinero necesario para un banco. _____

8. Lo contrario de *comprar*. _____

Las herramientas

9. Se usa para pintar las paredes. _____

10. Lo necesitamos para cortar la madera. _____

11. Es necesario usarlo para poner las puntillas. _____

12. Lo necesitamos para colocar el tornillo. _____

Un juego acróstico. *Translate the clues on the left from English into Spanish. (You do not need to include the articles.) Reading down the first letter of each word will then reveal a Spanish phrase.*

1. countertop ☐ __ __ __ __ __ __

2. dishwasher ☐ __ __ __ __ __ __ __ __

3. paper towel ☐ __ __ __ __ __ __ __ __ __ __

4. refrigerator ☐ __ __ __ __ __ __ __ __ __

5. to install ☐ __ __ __ __ __ __ __

6. towel ☐ __ __ __ __ __

7. urbanization ☐ __ __ __ __ __ __ __ __ __ __

8. to repair ☐ __ __ __ __ __ __

9. sideboard ☐ __ __ __ __ __ __ __

10. apron ☐ __ __ __ __ __

11. pot ☐ __ __ __

12. container ☐ __ __ __ __ __ __ __ __

13. title deed ☐ __ __ __ __ __ __ __ __ __ __ __ __ __ __ __ __

14. mirror ☐ __ __ __ __ __

15. garbage ☐ __ __ __ __ __

16. bottle opener ☐ __ __ __ __ __ __ __ __ __ __

17. frying pan ☐ __ __ __ __ __

18. uses ☐ __ __ __

19. clothes ☐ __ __ __

20. vacuum cleaner ☐ __ __ __ __ __ __ __ __

La respuesta vertical: _____

Palabras escondidas en este juego de puzle. *Find and circle the Spanish equivalents of these words hidden vertically, horizontally, and diagonally.*

```
                              D V
                            E B E D C Q
                          H H E A S B Y K K H
                        O Y D F O P P L J T B C B B
                      R N C R G C I P E L Z W F C K M I U
                    L X I W H I B Y S S R S K H O U F O X J N P
                  S P V E S T Í B U L O T E L C R C Y J X L L N R D
                  L U K N H C S V N V S A R Y S E H D V S I B N Z M
                  E B B O I S B N Z K D V E Z K I V G M U M F Z
                  R Z S       C V P L O I T Q Q L E       G M W
                  T B M       R T Y R R L H Q A L N       T A O
                  A A K       A V T X P L J T I O D       S N B
                  U K O       Q J I S Z E U J S A E       E T T
                  C O N T R A T O A S V T G S V U R L F D N A C
                  A Q R A D L Z X Y N T A T C I X U W B O C K X
                  W Q P S L Q N N K K G A A N N R B A N D E J A
                  A O U O R U A M A       X Y M R G N N I T
                  C R N E Q I F Q K       T U E Q F H D O R
                  S L R P H L B W X       C A I N J Q E Q E
                  J R D E T A U H U       O E Z Y V V R Z W
                  G Y G R G R C N V       I U R A B A N C O
                  G A J Q T L B E S       E H J R I Y L D N
                  O B I N O P A R R       Y V D Z A W W F G
                  R S L M M G V R I       A Z U C A R E R O
                  Q Q V K D E P R R       U P Q L K P G F X
```

alarm clock	knife	to tidy up
bench	lease	tray
blanket	to lock	to turn on
cup	napkin	view
door	to rent	wine
entrance	to sell	wineglass
housework	sugar bowl	

Crucigrama adivinanza. *Guess which word or phrase corresponds to each definition. Then fill in the crossword puzzle. (You do not need to include the articles.)*

Horizontales (*Across*)

5. Lo que usamos para secar la piel.

8. Utensilio para secar el pelo (*3 words*).

10. Utensilio para subir al armario.

12. Utensilio para poner el jabón.

13. Lugar para las medicinas en el baño.

14. Utensilio para colgar la ropa.

Verticales (*Down*)

1. Lugar para colocar la ropa sucia (*3 words*).

2. Recipiente para tomar el café y el té.

3. Lugar para colocar las medias y los calzoncillos (*underwear*) en el dormitorio.

4. Utensilio para barrer.

6. Para abrir el agua en la cocina (*3 words*).

7. Vaso para poner las flores.

9. Producto para refrescar el ambiente en casa.

11. Lugar para guardar los tenedores y las cucharas.

Traducción al inglés. *Try to guess what each phrase means and translate into English.*

1. el quinto piso _____

2. en casa _____

3. el balcón _____

4. subir y bajar _____

5. la toalla en el toallero _____

6. una copa de vino _____

7. la planta baja _____

8. se vende casa _____

9. el grifo de agua caliente _____

10. la mesa de comedor _____

11. se alquila apartamento _____

12. una cocina de gas _____

13. encender la lavadora _____

14. el desayuno _____

15. la mudanza _____

La comida

Food

En el supermercado

At the supermarket

VOCABULARIO

Advertising	**La publicidad**
ad	el anuncio
to advertise	anunciar
to appeal	atraer
appealing	atractivo, -a
brand	la marca
campaign	la campaña
catalog	el catálogo
discount coupon	el cupón de descuento
flyer	el volante
free	gratis
opening	la apertura
to persuade	persuadir
promotion	la promoción
Food stores	**Los establecimientos para comprar alimentos**
complaint box	el buzón de quejas
flea market	el mercado de pulgas
food	el alimento; la comida
open (adjective)	abierto, -a
to open	abrir
security guard	el/la guardia de seguridad
shopping basket	el cesto de la compra
shopping cart	el carrito de compras
shopping list	la lista de compras
suggestion box	el buzón de sugerencias
supermarket	el supermercado
taste	el sabor
tasting	la degustación
In the food store	**En las tiendas comestibles**
beer	la cerveza
cooking class	la clase de cocinar
entrance	la entrada
exit	la salida
fire exit	la salida de incendios
flower	la flor

In the food store (cont.)

flower shop	la florería; la floristería
nuts	las nueces
pharmacy	la farmacia
plastic bag	la bolsa plástica
wine	el vino

Buying and selling

bargain (noun)	la ganga
to bargain	negociar
cash register	la caja
cheap	barato, -a
to close	cerrar
closed	cerrado, -a
to cost	costar
costly	costoso, -a
expensive	caro, -a
free	gratis
inexpensive	barato, -a
merchandise	la mercancía
sale	la venta
to sell	vender
shop (noun), *store*	la tienda
to shop	comprar
to spend	gastar
teller, cashier	el cajero, la cajera

Customer service

bill	el billete
change	el cambio
credit card	la tarjeta de crédito
customer	el/la cliente
to help	ayudar
money	el dinero
to pay	pagar
payment	el pago
price	el precio
receipt	el recibo
return (noun)	la devolución
to return	devolver

Bakery and candy store

bread	el pan
cake	la torta
candy	los caramelos
chocolate	el chocolate
confectioner's, candy store	la confitería
cracker	la galleta
crusty	crujiente
fresh	fresco, -a
moldy	mohoso, -a
sweets	los dulces
toast (noun)	tostado, -a
to toast	tostar

En las tiendas comestibles (cont.)

Comprar y vender

El servicio al cliente

La panadería y la confitería

Butcher and delicatessen

beef	la carne
brisket	la falda
cheese	el queso
chicken	el pollo
chop	la chuleta
duckling	el pato
fillet	el filete
ham	el jamón
pork	el cerdo
pork loin	el lomo de cerdo
sausage	el chorizo
turkey	el pavo

Fish market

crab	el cangrejo
fish	el pescado
lobster	la langosta
mussel	el mejillón
oyster	la ostra
salmon	el salmón
sardine	la sardina
shrimp	el camarón
sole	el lenguado
squid	el calamar
trout	la trucha
tuna	el atún

Fruits and vegetables

apple	la manzana
apricot	el albaricoque
artichoke	la alcachofa
asparagus	el espárrago
avocado	el aguacate
banana	la banana; el plátano
beet	la remolacha
broccoli	el brócoli
carrot	la zanahoria
cauliflower	la coliflor
celery	el apio
corn	el maíz
cucumber	el pepino
eggplant	la berenjena
fig	el higo
garlic	el ajo
grape	la uva
grapefruit	el pomelo, la toronja
green bean	la judía verde
lemon	el limón
lettuce	la lechuga
mandarin orange	la mandarina
mango	el mango

La carnicería y el delicatessen

La pescadería

Las frutas y los vegetales

Fruits and vegetables (cont.)

melon	el melón
onion	la cebolla
orange	la naranja
pea	el guisante
peach	el durazno
pear	la pera
pepper	el pimiento
pineapple	la piña
plum	la ciruela
potato	la patata (Europe); la papa (Americas)
pumpkin	la calabaza
spinach	la espinaca
strawberry	la fresa
tomato	el tomate
vegetable	el vegetal
watermelon	la sandía
zucchini	el calabacín

Others foods and spices

almond	la almendra
bay leaf	la hoja de laurel
bean	el frijol
butter	la mantequilla
cereal	el cereal
coffee	el café
condiments	el condimento
egg	el huevo
flour	la harina
hazelnut	la avellana
honey	la miel
ice cream	el helado
margarine	la margarina
marmalade	la mermelada
mayonnaise	la mayonesa
milk	la leche
mustard	la mostaza
oats	la avena
oil	el aceite
olive	la oliva
oregano	el orégano
organic	orgánico, -a
paprika	el pimentón
peanut	el maní
pecan	la pacana
pepper	la pimienta
rice	el arroz
saffron	el azafrán
salt	la sal
seasoning	las especias
to spice	sazonar
sugar	el/la azúcar
tea	el té
vinegar	el vinagre
walnut	la nuez

Food preparation

to bake
to cook
to cut
grill
to measure
measuring cup
to peel
to roast
to sauté
spoon
to steam

La preparación para las comidas

hornear
cocinar
cortar
la parrilla
medir
la taza de medir
pelar
asar
saltear
la cuchara
cocinar al vapor

JUEGO 6·1

En el supermercado: Los vegetales. *In Spanish, write the word or phrase needed for each picture on the appropriate line. Include the article **el**, **la**, **los**, or **las** where necessary.*

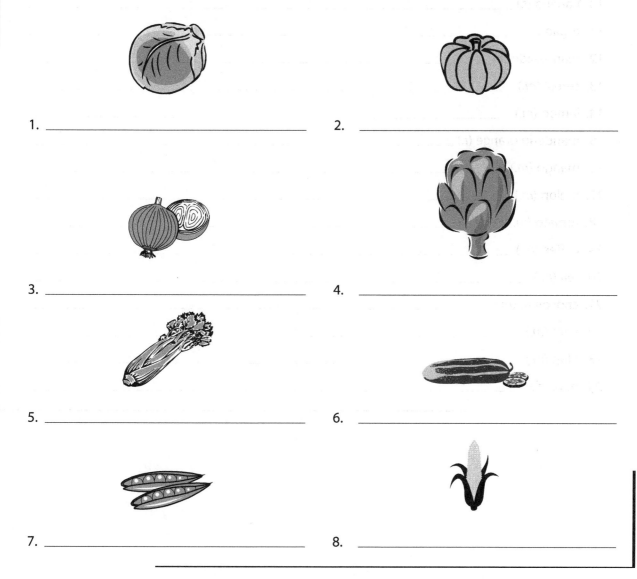

1. _____

2. _____

3. _____

4. _____

5. _____

6. _____

7. _____

8. _____

Cognados. *Translate these words from English into Spanish. Include the article **el** or **la** where necessary.*

1. to persuade _____

2. promotion (*f.*) _____

3. publicity (*f.*) _____

4. mayonnaise (*f.*) _____

5. mustard (*f.*) _____

6. potato (*f.*) _____

7. salmon (*m.*) _____

8. sardine (*f.*) _____

9. tuna (*m.*) _____

10. banana (*f.*) _____

11. organic _____

12. marmalade (*f.*) _____

13. cereal (*m.*) _____

14. lemon (*m.*) _____

15. mandarin orange (*f.*) _____

16. mango (*m.*) _____

17. melon (*m.*) _____

18. tomato (*m.*) _____

19. coffee (*m.*) _____

20. tea (*m.*) _____

21. chocolate (*m.*) _____

22. ham (*m.*) _____

23. fillet (*m.*) _____

24. olive (*f.*) _____

La publicidad y las compras. *Translate from English into Spanish and include the article **el**, **la**, **los**, or **las** as necessary.*

1. ad __ __ __ __ __ __ __ __ __

2. appealing (*m.*) __ __ __ __ __ __ __ __ __ __

3. free __ __ __ __ __ __

4. flyer __ __ __ __ __ __ __ __ __

5. to announce __ __ __ __ __ __ __ __

6. brand __ __ __ __ __ __ __

7. campaign __ __ __ __ __ __ __ __ __

8. opening __ __ __ __ __ __ __ __ __

9. catalog __ __ __ __ __ __ __ __ __

10. to close __ __ __ __ __ __

11. cheap (*f.*) __ __ __ __ __ __

12. costly (*m.*) __ __ __ __ __ __ __

13. shops __ __ __ __ __ __ __ __ __ __

14. to spend __ __ __ __ __ __

15. to appeal __ __ __ __ __ __

Selección múltiple. *Choose the best response for each question.*

1. En los mercados de alimentos podemos encontrar estas cosas excepto ...
   a. las flores.
   b. los periódicos.
   c. las revistas de moda.
   d. los techos.

2. Se puede comprar vino ...
   a. en la barbería.
   b. en línea.
   c. en un buzón.
   d. en lista de compras.

3. No se debe comer el pan cuando está ...
    a. tostado.
    b. crujiente.
    c. fresco.
    d. mohoso.

4. Una parte del pollo es ...
    a. la ostra.
    b. el ala.
    c. el durazno.
    d. la falda.

5. Es una fruta.
    a. el albaricoque
    b. la avellana
    c. la galleta
    d. el frijol

Un juego de palabras. *For each category below, choose the word or phrase that does not belong.*

1. **los panes están en** la entrada, la panadería, la salida, la farmacia

2. **la tienda de comestibles** la degustación, la clase de cocinar, el buzón de sugerencia, el diseño de moda

3. **la bebida** la cerveza, la leche, el vino, el lenguado

4. **las especias** la leche, el azafrán, el pimentón, la pimienta

5. **las grasas para cocinar** el apio, la mantequilla, el aceite, la margarina

6. **los dulces** los caramelos, los chocolates, las cebollas, las tortas

7. **las aves para comer** el pollo, el pato, el salmón, el pavo

8. **las nueces** la pacana, la avellana, la avena, la almendra

9. **la sazón** la mostaza, el azafrán, la hoja de laurel, la trucha

10. **la preparación para la comida** pelar, asar, saltear, vender

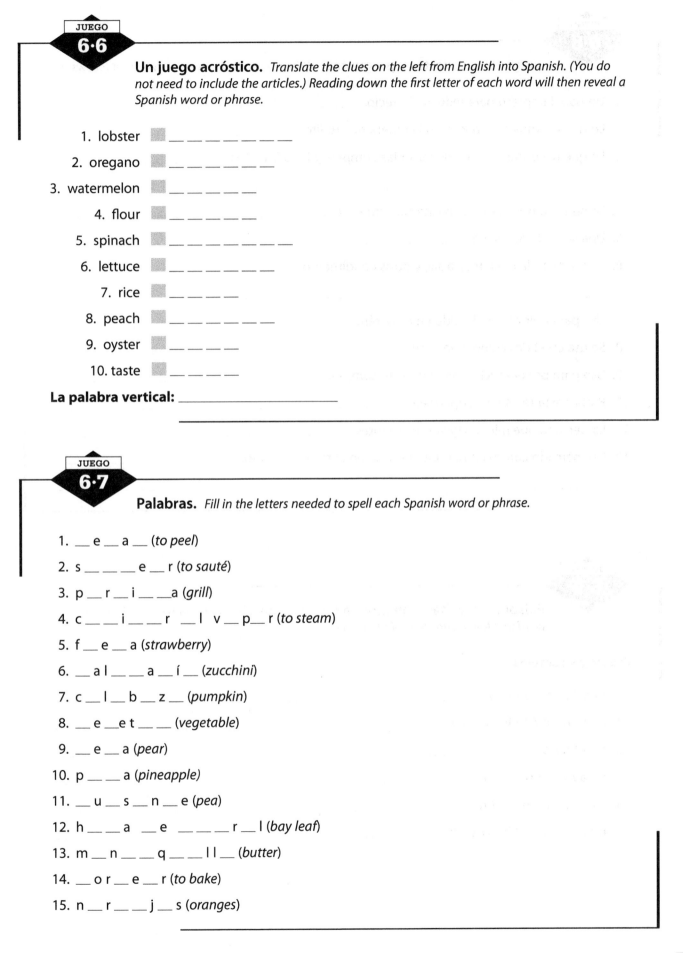

JUEGO
6·6

Un juego acróstico. *Translate the clues on the left from English into Spanish. (You do not need to include the articles.) Reading down the first letter of each word will then reveal a Spanish word or phrase.*

1. lobster ▨ __ __ __ __ __ __ __

2. oregano ▨ __ __ __ __ __ __

3. watermelon ▨ __ __ __ __ __

4. flour ▨ __ __ __ __ __

5. spinach ▨ __ __ __ __ __ __ __

6. lettuce ▨ __ __ __ __ __ __

7. rice ▨ __ __ __ __

8. peach ▨ __ __ __ __ __ __

9. oyster ▨ __ __ __ __

10. taste ▨ __ __ __ __

La palabra vertical: _____

JUEGO
6·7

Palabras. *Fill in the letters needed to spell each Spanish word or phrase.*

1. __ e __ a __ (*to peel*)

2. s __ __ __ e __ r (*to sauté*)

3. p __ r __ i __ __a (*grill*)

4. c __ __ i __ __ r __ l v __ p__ r (*to steam*)

5. f __ e __ a (*strawberry*)

6. __ a l __ __ a __ í __ (*zucchini*)

7. c __ l __ b __ z __ (*pumpkin*)

8. __ e __e t __ __ (*vegetable*)

9. __ e __ a (*pear*)

10. p __ __ a (*pineapple*)

11. __ u __ s __ n __ e (*pea*)

12. h __ __ a __ e __ __ __ __ r __ l (*bay leaf*)

13. m __ n __ __ q __ __ l l __ (*butter*)

14. __ o r __ e __ r (*to bake*)

15. n __ r __ __ j __ s (*oranges*)

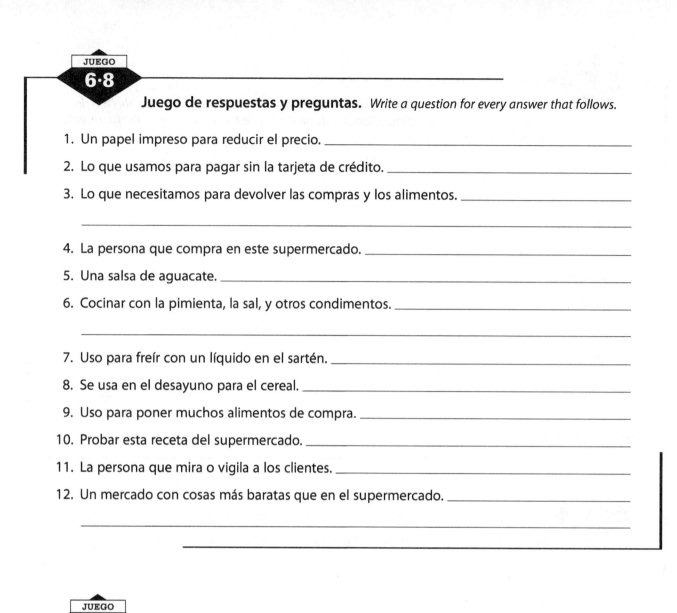

JUEGO 6·8

Juego de respuestas y preguntas. *Write a question for every answer that follows.*

1. Un papel impreso para reducir el precio. _____

2. Lo que usamos para pagar sin la tarjeta de crédito. _____

3. Lo que necesitamos para devolver las compras y los alimentos. _____
_____

4. La persona que compra en este supermercado. _____

5. Una salsa de aguacate. _____

6. Cocinar con la pimienta, la sal, y otros condimentos. _____
_____

7. Uso para freír con un líquido en el sartén. _____

8. Se usa en el desayuno para el cereal. _____

9. Uso para poner muchos alimentos de compra. _____

10. Probar esta receta del supermercado. _____

11. La persona que mira o vigila a los clientes. _____

12. Un mercado con cosas más baratas que en el supermercado. _____
_____

JUEGO 6·9

Palabras revueltas o anagrama de este capítulo. *Unscramble each Spanish word that follows and write it out correctly.*

Frutas y vegetales

1. r / o / l / c / i / f / o / l _____

2. r / a / n / o / z / h / a / i / a _____

3. g / i / h / o _____

4. o / a / t / r / n / o / j / _____

5. a / a / z / n / m / a / n _____

6. n / e / r / a / e / b / j / e / n _____

Saludables

7. a / f / h / a / c / l / c / a / o _____

8. i / l / e / m _____

9. e / r / l / m / a / h / c / o / a _____

10. i / b / ó / r / c / l / o _____

11. e / i / p / p / o / n _____

Ingredientes para cocinar

12. s / j / a / o _____

13. a / m / n / t / e / i / q / u / a / l / l _____

14. a / ú / z / a / c / r _____

15. g / n / i / a / v / e / r _____

JUEGO
6·10

Adivinanza. *Guess which word or phrase corresponds to each definition in Spanish.*

Los establecimientos para comprar alimentos tienen …

1. un lugar para escribir quejas (*complaints*). _____

2. muchos descuentos. _____

3. un lugar para hacer pan. _____

4. un departamento para encontrar las chuletas. _____

5. un lugar para pagar al salir del mercado. _____

6. un departamento para encontrar los mejillones y los cangrejos. _____

7. un lugar para comprar quesos. _____

8. un lugar para salir si hay fuego (*fire*). _____

9. una lista donde aparecen los precios bajos. _____

10. un lugar para pedir una torta de cumpleaños. _____

Palabras escondidas en este juego de puzle. *Find the hidden words and circle them vertically, horizontally, and diagonally.*

```
C T M R K B E C D Q V Q B P U F X
X Q Y L H S S X Z G M T S C I V T
Q K B Z Q D P U U F I P I K F D A
X Z E E S Q E K U U B I O Y Q S D
E I Y P K R C A C X A I I B E Q N
J U N X B X I F C D I J G R L Q N
B J C C M S A X O E P H F U Q X A
T C U O C Y S P E L I A F N Q G Y
L H T U C Y E N F O C T N F U F D
A G F K V I J A O H J S E H S R T
Y E S E F N N N Y U C R C F A I F
P H I A P A K A Q E J E L R L J F
T U H O L I U Y R V L W Q H T O V
A Q K L N D Ñ X W O U H D E E L X
Z K E W H H G A Z S C U C H A R A
A V C A L A B A C Í N H M X R N D
A Q G C I R U E L A F P K X Q S X
```

bean	hazelnut	plum	strawberry
to cook	lettuce	to sauté	zucchini
cup	oil	seasoning	
eggs	pineapple	spoon	

JUEGO

6·12

Palabras aprendidas. *Translate these words from English into Spanish. (You do not need to include articles.) Reading down the highlighted letters will then reveal a Spanish word.*

1. shopping list ■ ___ ___ ___ ___   ___ ___   ___ ___ ___ ___ ___ ___ ___
2. beer ___ ___ ___ ___ ___ ___ ■
3. fruit ■ ___ ___ ___ ___
4. pork loin ■ ___ ___ ___   ___ ___   ___ ___ ___ ___ ___
5. sausage ___ ___ ■ ___ ___ ___ ___
6. rice ___ ___ ■ ___ ___
7. wine ___ ■ ___ ___
8. salmon ■ ___ ___ ___ ___ ___
9. tuna ___ ■ ___ ___
10. asparagus ■ ___ ___ ___ ___ ___ ___ ___ ___
11. shrimp ___ ___ ___ ___ ■ ___ ___
12. peanut ___ ___ ___ ■
13. squid ___ ___ ___ ___ ___ ■ ___

La palabra vertical: ____________________

Crucigrama. *Fill in the crossword puzzle with the Spanish words.*

Horizontales (*Across*)

1. change
6. bargain
8. closed (*f.*)

10. price
12. free
13. sale

15. to advertise
17. bill
18. exit

Verticales (*Down*)

1. customer
2. merchandise
3. plastic
4. payment

5. opening
7. to measure
9. tasting
11. confectioner's, candy store

12. to spend
13. to sell
14. to open
16. to cost

Las compras y las tiendas

Shopping and stores

Las ropas y otros productos personales

Clothes and other personal items

VOCABULARIO

Shops / **Las tiendas**

beauty salon	la peluquería
bookstore	la librería
bridal shop	la tienda de novias
credit	el crédito
department store	los grandes almacenes
establishment	el establecimiento
fashion jewelry	la bisutería
furniture store	la mueblería
hardware store	la ferretería
hat shop	la sombrerería
ice cream parlor	la heladería
installment: on installment	a plazos
outlet store	la tienda de descuentos
to pawn	empeñar
pawn shop	la casa de empeño
perfumery	la perfumería
shoe store	la zapatería
shop (noun), store	la tienda
to shop	comprar
shopping center	el centro comercial
stationery store	la papelería
tailor's shop	la sastrería
upholstery shop	la tapicería
window	el escaparate
to wrap	envolver

In the department stores and clothing shops / **En los grandes almacenes y las tiendas de ropas**

bed sheet	la sábana
cloth	la tela
clothes	la ropa
corduroy	la pana
cotton	el algodón

In the department stores and clothing shops (cont.)

elevator	el elevador
fabric	la tela
fashion	la moda
to fit (someone)	quedarle bien
fitting room	el probador
garment	la prenda de vestir
gentleman's	el departamento de caballeros
hanger	el perchero
in fashion	de moda
lady's	el departamento de señoras
linen	el lino
linens	el departamento de la ropa de casa
loud	chillón, chillona
pillowcase	la funda de almohada
print	el estampado
to return	devolver
shelf, rack	el estante
silk	la seda
size	la talla
to take	llevar, llevarse
tight	estrecho, -a
to try on	probarse
velvet	el terciopelo

Colors and shapes

black	negro, -a
blue	azul
circle	el círculo
circular	circular
gold	dorado, -a
gray	gris
green	verde
indigo	índigo, -a
oval (noun)	el óvalo
oval (adjective)	ovalado, -a
pink	rosado, -a
purple	morado, -a
rectangle	el rectángulo
rectangular	rectangular
red	rojo, -a
round	redondo, -a
square	cuadrado, -a
triangle	el triángulo
triangular	triangular
white	blanco, -a
yellow	amarillo,-a

Clothes and more

Casual and formal attire

blouse	la blusa
bow tie	la pajarita
cap	la gorra

Casual and formal attire (cont.)

coat	el abrigo
dinner jacket	el traje de etiqueta
dress	el vestido
gown	el vestido largo
handkerchief	el pañuelo
hat	el sombrero
jacket	la chaqueta
jeans	los jeans
pants	los pantalones
raincoat	el impermeable
scarf	la bufanda
shirt	la camisa
skirt	la falda
suit	el traje
sun visor	la visera
sweatshirt	la sudadera
swimsuit	el bañador
tie	la corbata
T-shirt	la camiseta
tuxedo	el esmoquin
vest	el chaleco
wedding gown	el vestido de novia

La ropa informal y la ropa formal (cont.)

Undergarments and night clothes

house slippers	las zapatillas
lingerie	la lencería
pajamas	los pijamas
panties, women's underpants	el panty
pantyhose, stockings	las medias
robe	la bata de casa
shorts, men's underpants	los calzoncillos
sock	la media
tights	las mallas
undershirt	la camiseta

La ropa interior y la ropa de dormir

Shoes and accessories

bag	la bolsa
belt	el cinturón
boot	la bota
to buff, polish	lustrar
canvas shoe	la alpargata
glove	el guante
heel	el tacón
purse	el monedero, la bolsa
sandal	la sandalia
satchel	la cartera
shoe	el zapato; el calzado
shoelace	el cordón
shoe polish	el betún
sneakers	los tenis
sunglasses	las gafas de sol
umbrella	el paraguas; la sombrilla
wallet	la billetera

Los zapatos y los accesorios

Dry cleaning and alterations	La tintorería y los arreglos
to alter	arreglar
alteration	el arreglo
button	el botón
hole	el agujero
irregular	irregular
needle	la aguja
pocket	el bolsillo
scissors	la tijera, las tijeras
to sew	coser
spot	la mancha
tear	el desgarrón
thread	el hilo
to wash	lavar
zipper	el zíper

Jewelry	La joyería
bracelet	el brazalete
brooch	el broche
cuff links	los gemelos
diamond	el diamante
earring	el arete
emerald	la esmeralda
gold	el oro
jewel	la joya
jewelry	la joyería
necklace	el collar
ring	el anillo; la sortija
silver	la plata
watch	el reloj
wedding band	el anillo de casado, -a

Makeup and hair products	El maquillaje y los productos para el cabello
anti-wrinkle cream	la crema de antiarrugas
blusher	el colorete
cologne; eau de cologne	el agua de colonia; la colonia
dye (noun)	la tintura
to dye	teñir (el pelo)
eyebrow pencil	el lápiz de cejas
eyeliner	el lápiz de ojos
eye shadow	la sombra de ojos
face powder	los polvos de la cara
foundation makeup	la base
hand lotion	la crema para las manos
lipstick	el pintalabios
manicure	la manicura
mascara	el rímel
moisturizer	la crema hidratante
nail file	la lima de uñas
nail polish	el esmalte de uñas
nail polish remover	la acetona
perfume	el perfume
toilet water	el agua de colonia; la colonia
tweezers	las pinzas

Cognados. *Translate these words from English into Spanish; include the articles **el**, **la**, **los**, and **las** where necessary.*

1. cost (*m.*) _____

2. credit (*m.*) _____

3. elevator (*m.*) _____

4. cologne (*f.*) _____

5. perfume (*m.*) _____

6. lotion (*f.*) _____

7. angular _____

8. beige _____

9. perm (*m.*) _____

10. emerald (*f.*) _____

11. gel (*m.*) _____

12. triangle (*m.*) _____

13. triangular _____

14. violet (*m.*) _____

15. spray (*m.*) _____

16. shampoo (*m.*) _____

17. panties (*m.*) _____

18. shorts (*m.*) _____

19. uniform (*m.*) _____

20. manicure (*f.*) _____

21. pearl (*f.*) _____

22. ruby (*m.*) _____

23. sandal (*f.*) _____

24. jeans (*m.p.*) _____

25. rectangular _____

26. comfortable _____

27. elegant _____

28. circular _____

29. color (*m.*) _____

30. casual _____

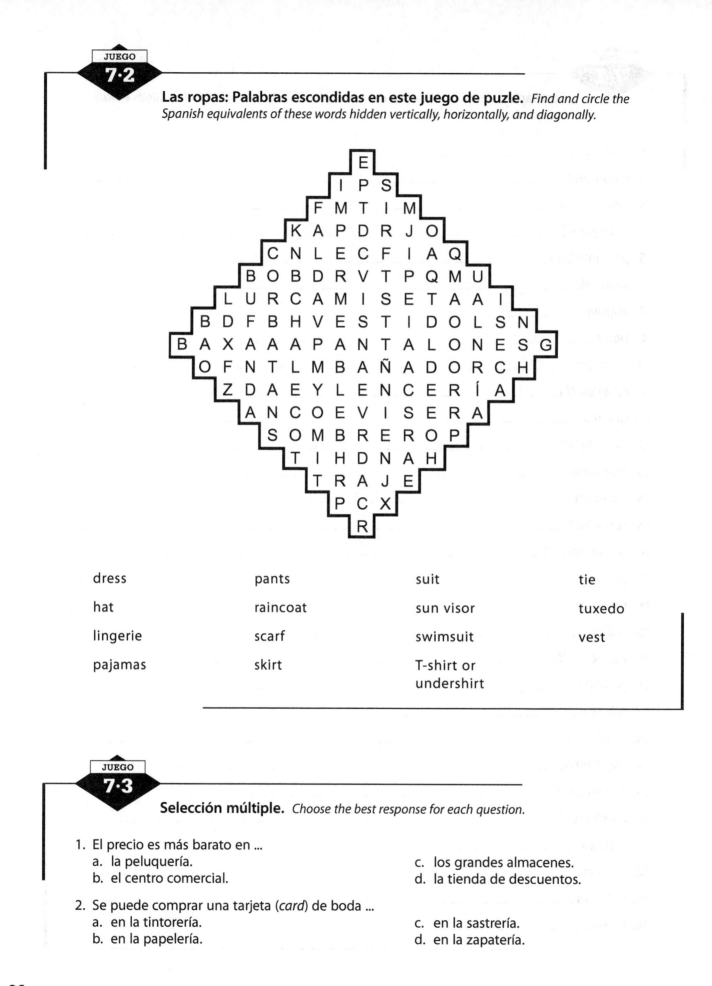

JUEGO

7·2

Las ropas: Palabras escondidas en este juego de puzle. *Find and circle the Spanish equivalents of these words hidden vertically, horizontally, and diagonally.*

```
            E
          I P S
        F M T I M
      K A P D R J O
      C N L E C F I A Q
      B O B D R V T P Q M U
    L U R C A M I S E T A A I
    B D F B H V E S T I D O L S N
  B A X A A A P A N T A L O N E S G
  O F N T L M B A Ñ A D O R C H
    Z D A E Y L E N C E R Í A
    A N C O E V I S E R A
      S O M B R E R O P
      T I H D N A H
        T R A J E
          P C X
            R
```

dress	pants	suit	tie
hat	raincoat	sun visor	tuxedo
lingerie	scarf	swimsuit	vest
pajamas	skirt	T-shirt or undershirt	

JUEGO

7·3

Selección múltiple. *Choose the best response for each question.*

1. El precio es más barato en …
   a. la peluquería.
   b. el centro comercial.
   c. los grandes almacenes.
   d. la tienda de descuentos.

2. Se puede comprar una tarjeta (*card*) de boda …
   a. en la tintorería.
   b. en la papelería.
   c. en la sastrería.
   d. en la zapatería.

3. En muchas zapaterías hay ...
   a. el betún.
   b. los pijamas.
   c. la camisa.
   d. las faldas.

4. Protegen las manos contra el frío.
   a. los calzoncillos
   b. los guantes
   c. las camisetas
   d. las zapatillas

5. El dinero se pone en ...
   a. el agujero.
   b. el remiendo.
   c. la billetera.
   d. la sombrilla.

Las compras. *Translate from English into Spanish; include the article **el**, **la**, **los**, or **las** where necessary.*

1. to dye __ __ __ __ __

2. mascara __ __ __ __ __ __ __

3. cuff links __ __ __ __ __ __ __ __ __ __

4. cap __ __ __ __ __ __ __

5. necklace __ __ __ __ __ __ __ __

6. sweatshirt __ __ __ __ __ __ __ __ __ __

7. blouse __ __ __ __ __ __ __

8. slippers __ __ __ __ __ __ __ __ __ __ __ __

9. pantyhose __ __ __ __ __ __ __ __ __

10. boots __ __ __ __ __ __ __ __

11. belt __ __ __ __ __ __ __ __ __ __

12. tights __ __ __ __ __ __ __ __ __

13. purse __ __ __ __ __ __ __ __ __

14. jacket __ __ __ __ __ __ __ __ __

15. robe __ __ __ __ __ __ __ __ __ __ __ __ __ __

Palabras aprendidas. *Translate these words from English into Spanish. (You do not need to include the articles.) Reading down the highlighted letters will then reveal a Spanish word or phrase.*

1. print ▊ _ _ _ _ _ _ _ _
2. loud (f.) _ _ _ ▊ _ _ _ _
3. cotton ▊ _ _ _ _ _ _
4. gloves ▊ _ _ _ _ _
5. handkerchief _ _ _ ▊ _ _ _
6. bow tie _ _ _ ▊ _ _ _ _
7. skirt _ _ _ ▊ _
8. emerald ▊ _ _ _ _ _ _ _ _
9. rectangle _ _ ▊ _ _ _ _ _ _
10. black (m.) _ _ _ _ ▊
11. circle _ _ _ _ _ ▊ _
12. pink (m.) _ _ _ _ _ ▊
13. white (m.) _ _ _ ▊ _ _
14. linen _ ▊ _ _
15. alteration ▊ _ _ _ _ _ _

La palabra vertical: _____

Un juego de palabras. *For each category below, choose the word or phrase that does **not** belong.*

1. **los bañadores son** ropa de etiqueta, ropa informal, ropa interior, ropa de dormir
2. **la gorra se usa para** ir a la boda, ir a la playa, caminar por la calle, proteger la cabeza
3. **la tintorería tiene** la tijera, la aguja, arreglos, los zapatos
4. **la ropa interior son** los calzoncillos, las zapatillas, las viseras, los calcetines
5. **la ropa formal es** el traje de etiqueta, el vestido largo, el escaparate, el esmoquin
6. **el accesorio es** el monedero, la mesa de noche, la billetera, el cinturón
7. **la lencería tiene** la alpargata, los pijamas, el panty, las medias
8. **el dinero se puede poner en** el bolsillo, la cartera, el pintalabios, la billetera
9. **las telas son** el lino, la pana, el algodón, la talla
10. **en la joyería se puede comprar** el broche, el botón, el brazalete, el diamante

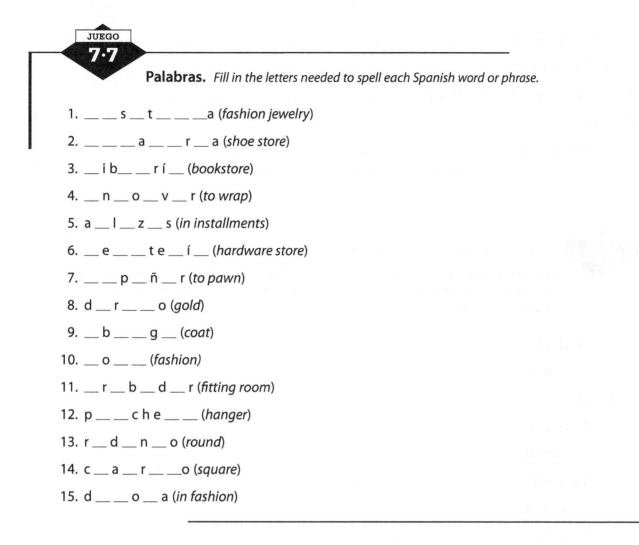

Palabras. *Fill in the letters needed to spell each Spanish word or phrase.*

1. __ __ s __ t __ __ __a (*fashion jewelry*)

2. __ __ __ a __ __ r __ a (*shoe store*)

3. __ i b__ __ r í __ (*bookstore*)

4. __ n __ o __ v __ r (*to wrap*)

5. a __ l __ z __ s (*in installments*)

6. __ e __ __ t e __ í __ (*hardware store*)

7. __ __ p __ ñ __ r (*to pawn*)

8. d __ r __ __ o (*gold*)

9. __ b __ __ g __ (*coat*)

10. __ o __ __ (*fashion*)

11. __ r __ b __ d __ r (*fitting room*)

12. p __ __ c h e __ __ (*hanger*)

13. r __ d __ n __ o (*round*)

14. c __ a __ r __ __o (*square*)

15. d __ __ o __ a (*in fashion*)

En las tiendas: Palabras revueltas o anagrama de este capítulo. *Unscramble each Spanish word below and write it out correctly.*

1. t / s / a / e / e / t / n _____

2. e / t / a / p / a / e / r / s / c / a _____

3. s / o / l / b / s / a _____

4. e / p / e / s / n / a / d / d / r / v / i / t / r / e (*3 words*) _____

5. r / s / t / o / j / i / a _____

6. s / j / a / y / o _____

7. a / g / s / a / f _____

8. a / l / l / o / n / i _____

9. r / e / j / g / a / u / o _____

10. ó / t / n / o / b _____

11. c / l / o / o / n / a / i _____

12. c / l / o / t / e / r / o / e _____

13. n / t / i / a / u / r / r / g / s / a / a _____

14. a / e / o / t / c / n / a _____

15. n / i / p / s / z / a _____

Un juego acróstico. *Translate the clues on the left from English into Spanish. (You do not need to include the articles.) Reading down the first letter of each word will then reveal a Spanish word or phrase.*

1. bookstore   __ __ __ __ __ __ __

2. gold   __ __ __

3. tailor's shop   __ __ __ __ __ __ __ __

4. to wrap   __ __ __ __ __ __ __

5. sandal   __ __ __ __ __ __ __

6. upholstery shop   __ __ __ __ __ __ __ __

7. ring   __ __ __ __ __

8. bracelet   __ __ __ __ __ __ __

9. wash   __ __ __ __

10. elevator   __ __ __ __ __ __ __

11. credit   __ __ __ __ __ __

12. irregular   __ __ __ __ __ __ __ __

13. furniture store   __ __ __ __ __ __ __ __

14. raincoat   __ __ __ __ __ __ __ __ __

15. tight (f.)   __ __ __ __ __ __ __

16. fiancée   __ __ __ __ __

17. velvet   __ __ __ __ __ __ __ __ __

18. eyes   __ __ __

19. silk   __ __ __ __

La palabra vertical: _____

Palabras escondidas en este juego de puzle. *Find and circle the Spanish equivalents of these words hidden vertically, horizontally, and diagonally.*

```
G E K A N Z L E Y H S V Y C K R X S R
M V P A R A G U A S X R F D R X N N H
I A F C M C A L Z A D O U Q Z B X R Q
U G N Z Í P E R T E R F H A P W J H A
B J O C C Y U O A Z M D I W E C S T T
O R L M H V E Z C P F M B A A Q A R Y
U X A J Y A K U Ó U W Z S N D L Z J S
O N E Z V Y D Q N C A Q F V P T U R S
P I N T A L A B I O S E R E M Z A E A
W F T I J L H V N C R T E D Y E T L S
P U N J T T E Ú L F M L J V X E S O Y
N Z O E V G T T P A S K D T R L E J L
W E J R O E H T E H E D L A F U F V M
J R D A B Y T T E H O Q H S I X R Z O
C H L S R U N C K Ñ K Y R K J L G C K
E L I S O C P O G L I K M P S N Q C T
S I W L N T O S A L G R X Z P A S K F
F A T X O V B E Q I C O R D Ó N S R U
Q J L X M C N R Y S H E L A T E M W T
```

bracelet	to sew	thread
to dye	shoe	umbrella
earrings	shoelace	watch
heel	shoe polish	zipper
lipstick	silver	
scissors	spot	

Los usos, los materiales y otros: Adivinanza. *Guess what Spanish word or phrase corresponds to each definition.*

1. La billetera en los pantalones _____

2. Se usa para pintar las uñas _____

3. Se usan para coser los botones _____

4. Se usa(n) para cortar la tela _____

5. El lugar donde se compran los perfumes _____

6. Se usa para protegerse del agua _____

7. Se usa para lustrar los zapatos _____

8. Se usan para proteger las manos del frío _____

9. Se trae para bañarse en la playa _____

10. Los colores de la bandera de los Estados Unidos _____

JUEGO

7·12

Juego de respuestas y preguntas. *Write a question for every answer given below.*

Las tiendas

1. La tienda donde compramos los helados. _____.

2. La tienda donde compramos el martillo y las puntillas. _____.

3. Un lugar donde puedes comprar la tela para los sofás. _____.

4. La tienda donde la novia compra su vestido para su día de boda. _____.

_____

La ropa y los zapatos

5. Algo que se debe hacer antes de comprar los zapatos. _____.

6. Compro esta blusa con esta talla. _____.

7. Cuando uno compra algo y regresa a casa con esta cosa. _____.

8. Cuando uno compra algo y después lo regresa a la tienda. _____.

_____

Más de las tiendas y compras

9. El departamento donde se compran sábanas. _____.

10. Lo que se uso para cubrir la almohada. _____.

11. El departamento de la tienda grande donde las señoras compran los vestidos. _____.

_____

12. La tienda donde compramos los sombreros. _____.

Las compras y las tiendas • Las ropas y otros productos personales 93

Crucigrama. *Fill in the crossword puzzle with the Spanish words.*

Horizontales (*Across*)

4. shoe
5. tweezers
7. manicure
8. purple (*m.*)

9. hanger
10. alteration
11. to wrap
12. fashion jewelry

15. fitting room
16. lingerie
17. department stores (*2 words*)
18. hole

Verticales (*Down*)

1. to sell
2. size
3. tear

6. pink (*f.*)
7. to measure
8. furniture store

11. window
13. heel
14. button

El transporte y la ciudad

Transportation and the city

VOCABULARIO

The neighborhood	El vecindario
avenue	la avenida
bridge	el puente
church	la iglesia
close	cerca, cerca de
dentist's office	la oficina del dentista
doctor's office	el consultorio médico
far	lejos
fence	la cerca
gated community	el barrio protegido
to help	ayudar
home insurance	el seguro de casa
lake	el lago
lamppost	el poste de luz
lawn	el césped
mesquite	la mezquita
neighbor	el vecino, la vecina
nursing home	la residencia de ancianos
office building	el edificio de oficinas
police station	la estación de policía
residence	la residencia
school	la escuela
street lighting	el alumbrado público
stroller	el coche de bebé
surroundings	los alrededores
vicinity	la cercanía

Transportation near home	El transporte cerca de casa
bicycle	la bicicleta, la bici
bus	el autobús; el bus
bus stop	la parada de autobuses
coach, bus	el autocar
ferryboat	el ferry
to get off	bajar, bajarse
to get on	subir
to get on the bus	subir al autobús
to give someone a ride	llevar a una persona
helmet	el casco
hybrid car	el carro híbrido

Transportation near home (cont.)

motorcycle	la moto
to pick up	recoger
pickup truck	el picop
public transportation	el transporte público
scooter (motorized)	el escúter
to stop	parar
subway	el metro, el subterráneo
subway station	la estación del metro
to take	tomar
to take the bus	tomar el autobús
taxi	el taxi
train	el tren
transportation	el transporte
truck	el camión
tunnel	el túnel
van	la furgoneta

Parts and functions of a car

to accelerate	acelerar
air conditioner	el aire acondicionado
auto	el carro; el auto
blinkers	las luces intermitentes
brake (noun)	el freno
to brake	frenar
to buckle	abrochar
to buckle up	abrochar (el cinturón del auto)
bumper	el parachoques
car alarm	la alarma (del auto)
car manual	el manual del auto
car rack	la baca
car sickness	el mareo
clutch	el embrague
control board	el tablero
cruise control	el control automático
door	la puerta
driver	el conductor, la conductora
driver's seat	el asiento del conductor, de la conductora
engine	el motor
gas tank	el tanque de gasolina
gear	la marcha
glove compartment	el guantero, la guantera
hood	el capó
horn	la bocina
ignition	la ignición
license plate	la matrícula; la placa
lights	las luces
mileage	el millaje
mirror	el espejo
passenger	el pasajero, la pasajera
passenger seat	el asiento del pasajero
pedal	el pedal
radiator	el radiador

Parts and functions of a car (cont.)

rearview mirror	el espejo retrovisor
right mirror	el espejo a la derecha
roof	el techo
seat	el asiento
speed (noun)	la velocidad
to speed	apurarse
to start	arrancar
steering wheel	el timón; el volante
tire	la llanta; el neumático
trunk	el maletero
valve	la válvula
window	la ventanilla
windshield	el parabrisas

Replacements and help for auto

battery cable	el cable (para cargar la batería)
brake fluid	el líquido de freno
car dealer	el distribuidor de autos
car maintenance	el mantenimiento del auto
to fill	llenar
to fill the tank	llenar el tanque de gasolina
filter (noun)	el filtro
gas filter	el filtro para la gasolina
gas station	la gasolinera
mechanic	el mecánico
to put gas in a car	poner gasolina
repair (noun)	la reparación
to repair	reparar
spark plug	la bujía
tow truck	la grúa

Traffic

accident	el accidente
block	la calle
car insurance	el seguro de auto
corner	la esquina
crash (noun)	el choque
to crash	chocar
to cross	cruzar
crossing	el cruce
dead-end street, cul-de-sac	la calle cerrada
detour	la desviación
to drive	manejar
driver	el chofer
electronic map	el mapa electrónico
fine	la multa
highway	la autopista
hill	la cuesta
lane	el carril
license	la licencia de manejar
park (noun)	el parque
to park	estacionar; parquear
parking (lot)	el aparcamiento; el estacionamiento

Las partes y las funciones del auto (cont.)

Los repuestos y la ayuda para el auto

El tráfico

Traffic (cont.)	El tráfico (cont.)
pedestrian	el peatón, la peatona
right	la derecha
road	la carretera
roundabout	la rotonda
to run over	atropellar
signal (noun)	la señal
to signal	señalar
stop sign	la señal de stop
toll	el peaje
traffic jam	el atasco; el embotellamiento
traffic light	el semáforo
traffic sign	la señal de tráfico
to turn	doblar
two-way street	la calle de dos sentidos
warning	el aviso

JUEGO 8·1

Cognados. *Translate these words from English into Spanish; include the articles **el**, **la**, **los**, and **las** where necessary.*

1. accident (*m.*) _____

2. bike (*f.*) _____

3. bus (*m.*) _____

4. insurance (*m.*) _____

5. convertible (*m.*) _____

6. rare (*m.*) _____

7. avenue (*f.*) _____

8. robot (*m.*) _____

9. bank (*m.*) _____

10. restaurant (*m.*) _____

11. hospital (*m.*) _____

12. clinic (*f.*) _____

13. mesquite (*f.*) _____

14. police station (*f.*) _____

15. synagogue (*f.*) _____

16. temple (*m.*) _____

17. train (*m.*) _____

18. vehicle (*m.*) _____

19. traffic (*m.*) _____

20. tunnel (*m.*) _____

21. to accelerate _____

22. alarm (*f.*) _____

23. motor (*m.*) _____

24. pedal (*m.*) _____

25. radiator (*m.*) _____

26. battery (*f.*) _____

27. to repair _____

28. gas (*f.*) _____

29. mechanic (*f.*) _____

30. to park _____

JUEGO 8·2

El transporte. *In Spanish, write the word or phrase needed for each picture on the appropriate line. For each answer, add the article **el** or **la** as necessary.*

1. _____ 2. _____

3. _____ 4. _____

5. _____ 6. _____

7. _____ 8. _____

Selección múltiple. *Choose the best response for each question.*

1. Este vecindario es caro porque es ...
   a. un estacionamiento libre.
   b. un poste de luz.
   c. un edificio instalado.
   d. un barrio protegido.

2. La guardería infantil (*day care*) es muy protegida porque cerca está ...
   a. la residencia de ancianos.
   b. la estación de policía.
   c. el consultorio de doctores.
   d. el edificio de oficinas.

3. En el auto o en el autobús vamos al otro barrio por ...
   a. el puente.
   b. los alrededores.
   c. la cercanía.
   d. las estaciones de autobuses.

4. ¡Vas muy rápido! Debes ...
   a. frenar.
   b. acelerar.
   c. subir.
   d. dormir.

5. Si no comprendo las partes del auto voy a ...
   a. abrochar el cinturón del auto.
   b. comprar un parabrisas.
   c. revisar el manual del auto.
   d. llenar el tanque de gasolina.

Las partes del auto. *Translate from English into Spanish; include the article **el**, **la**, **los**, or **las** where necessary.*

1. tire __ __ __ __ __ __ __ __ __
2. windshield __ __ __ __ __ __ __ __ __ __ __ __ __
3. trunk __ __ __ __ __ __ __ __ __ __ __
4. window __ __ __ __ __ __ __ __ __ __ __ __
5. roof __ __ __ __ __ __ __ __
6. seat __ __ __ __ __ __ __ __ __
7. steering wheel __ __ __ __ __ __ __ __
8. mirror __ __ __ __ __ __ __ __ __
9. lights __ __ __ __ __ __ __ __
10. glove compartment __ __ __ __ __ __ __ __ __ __ __
11. horn __ __ __ __ __ __ __ __
12. hood __ __ __ __ __ __ __
13. ignition __ __ __ __ __ __ __ __ __ __
14. gear __ __ __ __ __ __ __ __ __
15. bumper __ __ __ __ __ __ __ __ __ __ __ __ __

Un juego de palabras. *For each category below, choose the word or phrase that does **not** belong.*

1. **la calle está en** la ciudad, el vecindario, el barrio protegido, el manual del auto
2. **en la ciudad** la sinagoga, el templo, el embrague, la mezquita
3. **el reemplazo del auto** el filtro, el túnel, la bujía, la batería
4. **ir al trabajo en** el autobús, la furgoneta, el consultorio, la moto
5. **la parte del auto** el mareo, el freno, el tablero, la puerta
6. **la maleta está en** el maletero, el asiento, el volante, la baca
7. **las señales del tráfico** la gasolina, la rotonda, el cruce, la desviación
8. **los pagos del tráfico** la multa, el peaje, la cuesta, el pago
9. **los usos para viajar con el auto** el bulevar, el peatón, la calle, la autopista
10. **disfrutar (*enjoy*) en la ciudad** invitar a los amigos, ir al lago, viajar con amigos, encender el poste de luz

Un juego acróstico. *Translate the clues on the left from English into Spanish. (You do not need to include the articles.) Reading down the first letter of each answer will then reveal a Spanish word or phrase.*

1. blinkers __ __ __ __   __ __ __ __ __ __ __ __ __ __ __ __ __
2. to buckle __ __ __ __ __ __ __
3. crash __ __ __ __ __
4. to help __ __ __ __ __ __
5. lights __ __ __ __
6. tires __ __ __ __ __ __
7. mirror __ __ __ __ __ __
8. cruise control __ __ __ __ __ __ __ __ __ __ __ __ __ __
9. traffic jam __ __ __ __ __ __ __ __ __ __ __ __
10. roundabout __ __ __ __ __ __
11. to pick up __ __ __ __ __ __
12. highway __ __ __ __ __ __ __
13. to turn __ __ __ __ __
14. seats __ __ __ __ __ __

La palabra vertical: _____

Palabras. *Fill in the letters needed to spell each Spanish word or phrase. (You do not need to include articles.)*

1. __ a __ __ o __ í __ r __ __ o (*hybrid*)

2. i __ l __ s __ a (*church*)

3. __ l r __ d __ d __ r e __ (*surroundings*)

4. __ e r __ a (*fence*)

5. __ a __ __ n __ __ (*to walk*)

6. r __ c __ g __ r (*to pick up*)

7. a __ __ l __ r __ r (*to accelerate*)

8. p __ r __ __ (*to stop*)

9. __ ú __ e __ (*tunnel*)

10. __ __ e __ o (*brake*)

11. __ i __ l __ j __ (*mileage*)

12. p __ s __ __ e __ a (*passenger*)

13. a __ r __ __ c __ r (*to start*)

14. m __ l __ t __ r __ (*trunk*)

15. g __ __ a (*tow truck*)

Palabras revueltas o anagrama de este capítulo. *Unscramble each Spanish word below and write it out correctly.*

El transporte

1. ó / c / m / a / n / i _____

2. í / c / r / a / e / n / c / a _____

3. á / t / e / r / r / s / u / n / b / o / e _____

4. g / o / u / f / r / e / t / a / n _____

5. c / i / p / p / o _____

6. a / t / c / o / u / r / a _____

El tráfico

7. r / c / u / e / c _____

8. a / r / c / r / l / i _____

9. r / a / c / t / e / r / r / e / a _____

10. a / r / t / o / e / a / l / l / p / r _____

11. c / n / o / u / d / c / o / t / r _____

Las partes del auto

12. ó / n / m / i / t _____

13. s / a / s / i / r / b / a / r / a / p _____

14. í / r / t / a / m / a / l / u / c _____

15. a / r / a / p / s / e / u / o / q / h / c _____

JUEGO 8·9

Palabras aprendidas. *Translate these words from English into Spanish. Reading down the highlighted letters will then reveal a Spanish word or phrase.*

1. to park ▓ __ __ __ __ __ __ __ __

2. to accelerate __ __ __ ▓ __ __ __ __

3. vehicle ▓ __ __ __ __ __ __ __

4. mirror ▓ __ __ __ __ __

5. helmets __ __ __ ▓ __ __

6. trucks __ __ __ ▓ __ __ __

7. glove compartment __ __ __ ▓ __ __ __

8. dealer ▓ __ __ __ __ __ __ __ __ __

9. alarm __ __ ▓ __ __ __

10. to put gas into a car __ __ __ __ ▓ __ __ __ __ __ __

11. mechanic __ __ __ __ __ ▓ __ __

12. gas filter __ __ __ __ __ ▓ __ __ __ __ __ __ __ __

La respuesta vertical: _____

Palabras escondidas en este juego de puzle. *Find and circle the Spanish words hidden horizontally, vertically, and diagonally.*

```
M X G P C N E U M Á T I C O O Q U Z I K X
X I A C F Q H F Z A X J A V C T I O P I F
M T S W T Y T F X J Q F I B R T M P E L H
I P O R E V Z F J T P S T O B Q T J A Q X
K E L Y E K J L L B Y D J V Y J V F T S O
W L I F J S G G B A M M P U A G A K Ó Q I
V R N P O P I W N O N L K Z Q T H X N K R
E M E M V O D D F E O D F G L V T L N O M
C N R K W J O F E N H D A U B A M T R V N
I F A D N T B J A N N A M P F E F T N Z V
N Q S A B Y L I B Ó C A Y I I D L E L D E
O O A L R X A V I L N I V F R I O V J B L
W A Q U O S R C E I X U A J F U O G V T O
U X Y S C D A E U N C S O Y H X D E T G C
F S B E E I T Q P N T H R J S B Q C Z G I
R W T P V V S Q M A V A O A T A S C O B D
J T S S Y E U X U V R N N Q R V Q F F P A
O É E Y Y L G K A F V A L I U Z I U N E D
C D X N U W I G I Y W N R A L E I M S A C
A V H I A X S Z B H N A Q J G L C Y K J D
T N I Y X J H E S X H J O A H O A D D E U
```

corner	lake	speed
crash	lawn	tire
detour	neighbor (*m.*)	toll
filter	pedestrian (*m.*)	traffic jam
fine	to repair	to turn
gas station	residence	window

Adivinanza: El vecindario y otros. *Guess what Spanish word or phrase corresponds to each definition given below.*

1. Algo para proteger la cabeza en la moto _____

2. Algo para alumbrar a toda la ciudad _____

3. Algo para parar al auto _____

4. Algo para llevar al bebé a un paseo _____

5. Algo para salir del auto _____

6. Como llevar a una persona que no puede caminar mucho. _____

7. Algo para mirar el auto atrás _____

8. Algo que tiene tres colores: rojo, amarillo y verde _____

9. El lugar para guardar la maleta en el auto _____

10. Un lugar para tener una cita con un médico _____

JUEGO
8·12

Juego de respuestas y preguntas. *Write a question for every answer given below.*

El vecindario

1. Esta persona maneja su taxi. _____.

2. Un paciente va a este lugar para revisar los dientes. _____.

3. Una comunidad protegida por la seguridad. _____.

4. Este es un lugar para educar a los niños. _____.

El tráfico

5. Este es el uso para avisar con sonido en el auto. _____.

6. Esto es para revisar las calles, los números de casas y otros. _____.

7. Esta persona cruza de una calle a la otra. _____.

8. Este es el documento necesario para manejar el auto. _____.

Las compras y más

9. El lugar donde puedo comprar la gasolina para mi auto. _____.

10. El lugar donde puedo comprar un auto de este año. _____.

11. El hecho de revisar el líquido de freno, el filtro del aire acondicionado y más. _____.

_____

12. Lo que usamos en caso de accidente para cargar la batería. _____.

Crucigrama. *Fill in the crossword puzzle with the Spanish words.*

Horizontales (*Across*)

2. bridge
3. to help
4. train
5. warning

7. far
8. valve
10. car sickness
11. right

12. windshield
15. radiator
16. horn
17. repair

Verticales (*Down*)

1. window
2. pedal
5. to accelerate

6. street
9. hill
10. map

11. detour
13. engine
14. to speed

Los viajes y el turismo

Travel and tourism

VOCABULARIO

Travel arrangements	Los preparativos para viajes
agent	el/la agente
to arrange	preparar
arrangement	el preparativo
to book a flight	hacer una reserva para un vuelo
to book a room	hacer una reserva para un hotel
credit card	la tarjeta de crédito
electronic reservation	la reserva electrónica
fare	el pasaje
journey	el viaje
map	el mapa
plan (noun)	el plan
to plan	planear
to print	imprimir
promotion	la promoción
to rent a car	alquilar un auto
reservation	la reserva
schedule	el horario
to schedule	programar
ticket	el boleto
travel (noun)	el viaje
to travel	viajar
travel agency	la agencia de viajes
travel agent	el/la agente de viajes
traveler	el pasajero, la pasajera; el viajero, la viajera
traveler's check	el cheque de viajero
trip	el viaje

Tourism	El turismo
bon voyage	buen viaje
brochure	el folleto
complaint	la queja
to enjoy	disfrutar de
excursion	la excursión
exotic	exótico, -a
guide	el/la guía
guided tour	la visita guiada
hitchhiking	el autostop
package tour	el viaje organizado
season	la temporada
site	el lugar

Tourism (cont.)

tour (noun)	el tour
to tour	hacer un tour
tourist	el/la turista
travel guide	la guía turística
vacation	las vacaciones

Traveling abroad

abroad	en el extranjero
border	el borde; la frontera
currency	la moneda
currency exchange office	la oficina de cambios de moneda
customs	la aduana
to declare	declarar
duty	el impuesto
duty free	libre de impuesto
exchange	el cambio de moneda
tax	el impuesto
tourist card	la tarjeta de turista
tunnel	el túnel

Air travel

airline	la aerolínea
airline miles	millas aéreas
airport	el aeropuerto
arrival	la llegada
availability	la disponibilidad
available	disponible
available seat	el asiento disponible
baggage	el equipaje
boarding	el embarque
bonus	el bono
cancellation	la cancelación
charge	el cargo
checked	facturado, -a
to check in	registrarse
to complain	quejarse
control	el control
delay (noun)	el retraso
to delay	retrasar
departure	la salida
to disembark	desembarcar
domestic flight	el vuelo nacional
escalator	la escalera mecánica
flight	el vuelo
full flight	el vuelo lleno
gate	la puerta de embarque
hand luggage	el equipaje de mano
helicopter	el helicóptero
international flight	el vuelo internacional
to land	aterrizar
landing	el aterrizaje

El turismo (cont.)

Viajar al extranjero

Viajes en avión

Air travel (cont.)

layover	la escala
load (noun)	la carga
to load	cargar
luggage	el equipaje
meal service	el servicio de comida
nonstop flight	el vuelo directo
on schedule	a la hora prevista
parking	el aparcamiento; el estacionamiento
passenger	el pasajero, la pasajera
reception	la recepción
to complain	quejarse
reward	la recompensa
round trip ticket	el billete de ida y vuelta
runway	la pista
security	el control de seguridad
standby list	la lista de espera
stopover (noun)	la escala
to stop over	hacer una escala
suitcase	la maleta
takeoff (noun)	el despegue
to take off	despegar
ticket agent	el agente, la agente
ticket counter	el mostrador

On the plane

air pressure	la presión del aire
airsickness	el mareo
airsickness bag	la bolsa para el mareo
aisle	el pasillo
altitude	la altura
blanket	la manta; la frazada
cabin class	la clase turista
cockpit	la cabina del piloto
copilot	el/la copiloto
crew	la tripulación
duration	la duración
economy class	la clase turista
emergency exit	la salida de emergencia
to fasten	abrocharse
to fasten seatbelts	abrocharse los cinturones
to fit	caber
flight attendant	el/la asistente de vuelo
to fly	volar
headset	los auriculares
lavatory	el servicio; el baño
life jacket	el chaleco salvavidas
main cabin	la cabina principal
no smoking	no fumar
on board	a bordo
overhead compartment	el compartimiento superior
pillow	la almohada
pilot	el/la piloto

Viajes en avión (cont.)

En el avión

On the plane (cont.)

rear of the plane	la parte trasera del avión
row	la fila
seat	el asiento
seatbelt	el cinturón de seguridad
speed	la velocidad
turbulence	la turbulencia

Travel by train

berth	la litera
bullet train	el tren bala
cabin	la cabina
cable car	el tranvía
daytime train	el tren diurno
dining room	el comedor
high-speed train	el tren de alta velocidad
locomotive	la locomotora
platform	el andén
shuttle bus	el servicio de enlace
train conductor	el revisor, la revisora
train restaurant	el coche comedor
train station	la estación de los trenes

Travel by ship

captain	el capitán
cruise	el crucero
deck	la cubierta
dock (noun)	el muelle
to dock	atracar
to float	flotar
harbor	la bahía
lifeboat	el bote salvavidas
lifesaver	el salvavidas
ocean liner	el trasatlántico
overboard	por la borda
port	el puerto
river cruise	el crucero fluvial
rough sea	la marejada
sea	el mar
seaman	el marinero
seaport	el puerto marino
seasick	mareado, -a
ship	el buque
storm	la tormenta
tide	la marea
transoceanic	transoceánico, -a
transoceanic travel	el viaje transoceánico

Accommodations

to accommodate	acomodar
amenities	los servicios
bed and breakfast	el alojamiento y desayuno

En el avión (cont.)

Viajar en tren

Viajar en barco

Los alojamientos

Accommodations (cont.)	Los alojamientos (cont.)
to book	reservar
camper	la caravana
to disturb	molestar
guest	el/la huésped
hostel	el albergue
inn	la posada
mobile home	la casa móvil
motel	el motel
RV	la autocaravana, la caravana
tent	la tienda de campaña

At the hotel	En el hotel
bellboy	el botones
to check out	abandonar el hotel; pagar
double room	la habitación doble
first rate	de primera categoría
freight elevator	el montacargas
laundry service	el servicio de lavandería
rate per day, daily rate	el precio de cada día
reception	la recepción
room	la habitación
room service	el servicio de habitaciones
vacant	disponible
vacant room	la habitación disponible

JUEGO 9·1

Palabras aprendidas. *Translate these words from English into Spanish; include the article **el, la, los,** or **las** as necessary.*

1. to fasten seatbelts _____

2. emergency exit (*f.*) _____

3. to fasten _____

4. tunnel (*m.*) _____

5. exit (*f.*) _____

6. mile (*f.*) _____

7. wheelchair (*f.*) _____

8. traveler's check (*m.*) _____

9. travel agency (*f.*) _____

10. agent (*f.*) _____

11. sea (*m.*) _____

12. motel (*m.*) _____

13. seat (*m.*) _____

14. seatbelt (*m.*) _____

15. speed (*f.*) _____

16. window (*f.*) _____

17. parking (*m.*) _____

18. passenger (*m.*) _____

19. promotion (*f.*) _____

20. blanket (*f.*) _____

21. price (*m.*) _____

22. to rent _____

23. currency (*f.*) _____

24. control (*m.*) _____

JUEGO
9·2

Cognados. *Translate these words from English into Spanish; include the articles **el, la, los**, and **las** as necessary.*

1. tourist (*m.*) _____

2. immigration (*f.*) _____

3. immunization (*f.*) _____

4. passport (*m.*) _____

5. visa (*f.*) _____

6. jet (*m.*) _____

7. security (*f.*) _____

8. terminal (*f.*) _____

9. plan (*m.*) _____

10. helicopter (*m.*) _____

11. exotic (*m.*) _____

12. tour (*m.*) _____

13. airport (*m.*) _____

14. reception (*f.*) _____

15. to plan _____

16. cabin (*f.*) _____

17. pilot (*f.*) _____

18. turbulence (*f.*) _____

19. train (*m.*) _____

20. yacht (*m.*) _____

21. comfortable _____

22. reception (*f.*) _____

23. suite (*f.*) _____

24. to declare _____

25. captain (*m.*) _____

26. to float _____

27. port (*m.*) _____

28. hotel (*m.*) _____

29. service (*m.*) _____

30. international (*m.*) _____

JUEGO

9·3

Selección múltiple. *Choose the best response or completion for each item.*

1. Las personas que tienen mucho dinero prefieren ...
   a. estar en un hotel barato.
   b. los servicios malos.
   c. estar en primera categoría.
   d. las comidas muy malas.

2. Los viajes en barco tienen ...
   a. el bote salvavidas.
   b. el despegue.
   c. el vuelo nacional.
   d. el aterrizaje.

3. En los aviones tienen ...
   a. la clase turista.
   b. la casa móvil.
   c. el puerto marino.
   d. el alojamiento.

4. La autocaravana aparece en ...
   a. el motel.
   b. el puerto marino.
   c. el crucero fluvial.
   d. el revisor.

5. La parte del aeropuerto es ...
   a. la playa y la arena.
   b. la nube nublada.
   c. la biblioteca pública.
   d. la pista de aterrizaje.

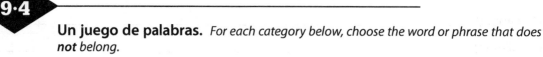

JUEGO 9·4

Un juego de palabras. *For each category below, choose the word or phrase that does not belong.*

1. **lo que se necesita para viajar** la maleta, los zapatos, el iPad, la cama

2. **el pago para los viajes** la llegada, el dinero, la tarjeta de crédito, la moneda

3. **los preparativos para viajar** la reserva de un agente, el horario, la reserva electrónica, el mareo

4. **el documento para ir a un país extranjero** el pasaporte, la visa, el baño, la evidencia

5. **los aviones tienen** la tripulación, el piloto, la cabina, el barco

6. **los viajes en barcos necesitan** el capitán, el puente, el muelle, la caravana

7. **los alojamientos aparecen en** la posada, la tienda de campaña, el botones, el albergue

8. **los hoteles tienen** el precio de cada día, el servicio de lavandería, la habitación doble, el trasatlántico

9. **los trenes** el tren de alta velocidad, la estación de trenes, el aeropuerto, la litera

10. **el turismo tiene** el folleto, la visita guiada, el tour, la marea

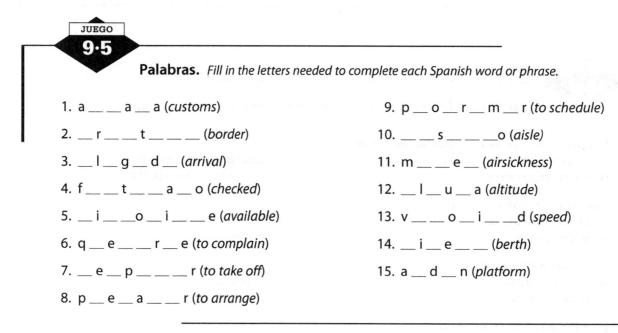

JUEGO 9·5

Palabras. *Fill in the letters needed to complete each Spanish word or phrase.*

1. a __ __ a __ a (*customs*)

2. __ r __ __ t __ __ __ __ (*border*)

3. __ l __ g __ d __ (*arrival*)

4. f __ __ t __ __ a __ o (*checked*)

5. __ i __ o __ i __ __ e (*available*)

6. q __ e __ __ r __ e (*to complain*)

7. __ e __ p __ __ __ __ r (*to take off*)

8. p __ e __ a __ __ __ r (*to arrange*)

9. p __ o __ r __ m __ r (*to schedule*)

10. __ __ s __ __ __ o (*aisle*)

11. m __ __ e __ (*airsickness*)

12. __ l __ u __ a (*altitude*)

13. v __ __ o __ i __ __ d (*speed*)

14. __ i __ e __ __ (*berth*)

15. a __ d __ n (*platform*)

Los viajes y frases para los viajes. *Translate from English into Spanish; include the articles **el, la, los,** and **las** as necessary.*

1. boarding __ __ __ __ __ __ __ __ __ __

2. charge __ __ __ __ __ __ __

3. delay __ __ __ __ __ __ __ __ __

4. disembark __ __ __ __ __ __ __ __ __ __ __

5. full flight __ __ __ __ __ __ __ __ __ __ __

6. package tour __ __ __ __ __ __ __ __ __ __ __ __ __

7. gate __ __ __ __ __ __ __ __ __ __ __ __ __ __

8. enjoy __ __ __ __ __ __ __ __

9. airline miles __ __ __ __ __ __ __ __ __ __

10. domestic flight __ __ __ __ __ __ __ __ __ __ __ __

11. excursion __ __ __ __ __ __ __ __ __ __

12. destiny __ __ __ __ __ __ __ __ __

13. credit card __ __ __ __ __ __ __ __ __ __ __ __ __

14. travel __ __ __ __ __ __

15. guided tour __ __ __ __ __ __ __ __ __ __ __

16. tax __ __ __ __ __ __ __ __ __

17. available seat __ __ __ __ __ __ __ __ __ __ __ __ __ __

18. landing __ __ __ __ __ __ __ __ __ __

19. load __ __ __ __ __ __ __

20. non-stop flight __ __ __ __ __ __ __ __ __ __ __

21. on schedule __ __ __ __ __ __ __ __ __ __ __

22. round trip ticket __ __ __ __ __ __ __ __ __ __ __ __ __ __ __ __

23. reward __ __ __ __ __ __ __ __ __ __

24. ticket counter __ __ __ __ __ __ __ __ __ __ __

25. runway __ __ __ __ __ __ __

26. air pressure __ __ __ __ __ __ __ __ __ __ __ __ __ __

Palabras escondidas en este juego de puzle. *Find and circle the Spanish words hidden vertically, horizontally, and diagonally.*

```
N D J F Z Y E C A J E T N Z K F U W R
H U X F W Y H I J T T E H T Q C U K A
T S E F R V Y O N K K O H W G Z B Z U
E P V Y Y A K E R L Z L Y O V X O N X
M Z Z N J I G G U A Q M T K W S Y H X
P N H U M A G G Q O R E F Z U C C N G
O D I S P O N I B I L I D A D X K K M
R J T D Y M F E L L I C O D X I G X H
A H F I C A J W O R Y J C Z Z S C P D
D R U W T A L F C B S A L I D A C A V
A K Y J P B V T O O G S L L W O M S A
H S N I D M P W M F P C H I K R D A C
O M U K J O L F O S G I W W E R Í J A
A Q E I P X K U T D W D L D Z U Q E C
E N U G Y J S A O C M K Q O G Z A R I
Z O A L D C K D R T L Z J U T Z Y O O
X H A G T H T R A N V Í A Q E O J M N
Z V F R A G R S A T U E B V U J G G E
O J J I G Z C O M E D O R R I P A D S
```

agent	copilot (*m.*)	luggage
availability	dining room	passenger (*m.*)
brochure	exit	schedule
cable car	guide	season
complaint	locomotive	vacation

Los viajes: Adivinanza. *Guess what Spanish word or phrase corresponds to each definition or description.*

1. Para guardar la ropa _____

2. Para poder subir al avión _____

3. Para vomitar en el avión _____

4. Para pasar al baño en el avión _____

5. Para poder escuchar la música en el avión _____

_____

6. Para poner objetos personales arriba del asiento _____

_____

7. La parte de atrás del avión _____

8. Viaje en un buque de un continente a otro _____

_____

9. Las personas que llevan el desayuno a la habitación del hotel _____

_____

10. Para subir al quinto piso del hotel _____

Crucigrama. *Fill in the crossword puzzle with the Spanish words.*

Horizontales (*Across*)

3. duty

5. airline

6. fare

7. to check in

10. cabin

12. site

13. to print

16. bonus

17. turbulence

Verticales (*Down*)

1. to land

2. guest (*m./f.*)

4. train

8. crew

9. bon voyage
   (*2 words*)

11. arrangement

14. to fit

15. row

16. lavatory

JUEGO 9·10

Un juego acróstico. *Translate the clues on the left from English into Spanish. (You do not need to include the articles.) Reading down the first letter of each word will then reveal a Spanish word or phrase.*

1. luggage   ▨ _ _ _ _ _ _ _

2. berth   ▨ _ _ _ _ _ _

3. map   ▨ _ _ _

4. currency exchange office   ▨ _ _ _ _ _ _ _ _ _ _ _ _ _

5. no smoking   ▨ _   _ _ _ _ _

6. tourist card   ▨ _ _ _ _ _ _ _ _ _ _ _ _

7. customs   ▨ _ _ _ _ _

8. cancellation   ▨ _ _ _ _ _ _ _ _ _

9. seat   ▨ _ _ _ _ _ _

10. electronic reservation   ▨ _ _ _ _ _ _ _ _ _ _ _ _ _ _ _

11. travel guide   ▨ _ _ _ _ _ _ _ _ _ _

12. hitchhiking   ▨ _ _ _ _ _ _ _

13. departure   ▨ _ _ _ _ _

La palabra vertical: _____

Viajar en barco: Palabras escondidas en este juego de puzle. *Find and circle the Spanish words hidden vertically, horizontally, and diagonally.*

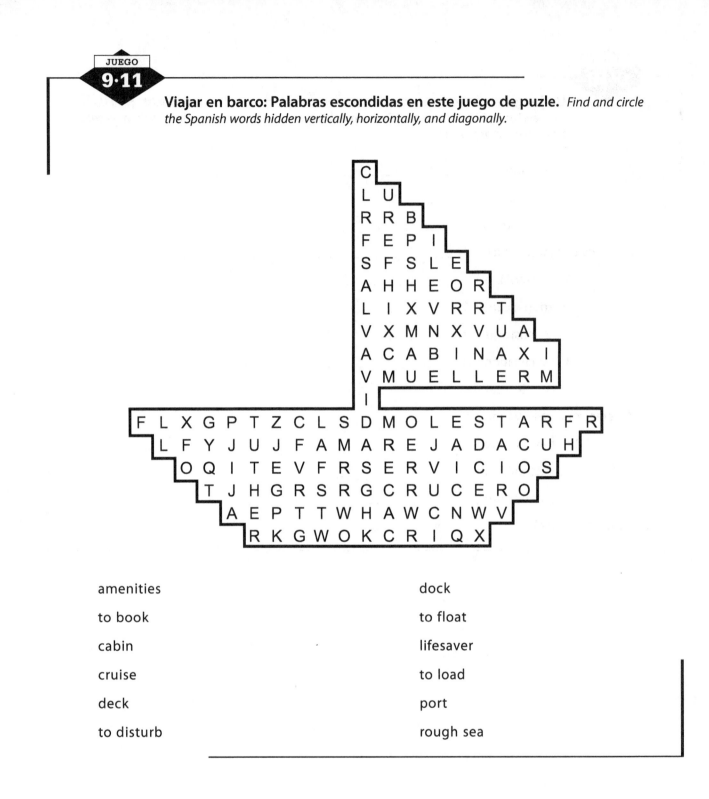

amenities	dock
to book	to float
cabin	lifesaver
cruise	to load
deck	port
to disturb	rough sea

El tiempo libre, la diversión y el entretenimiento

Free time, fun, and entertainment

Free time, fun, and entertainment

to amuse (oneself)
amusing
casino
chat
to date
to have a good time
to have fun
to hum
joke (noun)
to joke
to laugh
laughter
leisure
to play
puzzle
to relax
to visit

El tiempo libre, la diversión y el entretenimiento

entretener, entretenerse
entretenido, -a
el casino
el chat
salir con un amigo, una amiga
pasarlo bien
divertirse
canturrear
la broma
bromear
reír, reírse
la risa
el ocio
jugar
el puzle
relajarse; descansar
visitar

Leisure for children and adults

amusement park
carousel
children's literature
comic book store
comic strip
computer games
digital camera
doll
to draw
drawing
fairy tale
to glide
to play
puppet
roller coaster
scooter
skateboard
teen fiction
toy (noun)

El tiempo libre para los niños y los adultos

el parque de diversiones
los caballitos; el tiovivo
la literatura infantil
la tienda de los cómicos
el comic
los juegos de computadora
la cámara digital
la muñeca
dibujar
el dibujo
el cuento de hadas
deslizarse
jugar
el títere
la montaña rusa
el patinete
el monopatín
la literatura juvenil
el juguete

Leisure for children and adults (cont.)

video	el vídeo
video camera	la videocámara
video game	el videojuego

Music and dance

auditorium	el auditórium
castanets	las castañuelas
choir, chorus	el coro
dance (noun)	el baile
to dance	bailar
to go to a dance	salir a bailar
group	el conjunto
to play an instrument	tocar un instrumento
to sing	cantar
song	la canción
voice	la voz

Cinema, television, and theater

to applaud	aplaudir
applause	el aplauso
award	el premio
box office	la taquilla
comedy	la comedia
comical	cómico, -a
curtain	el telón
drama	el drama
dramatic	dramático, -a
ending	el final
exciting	emocionante
flop	el fracaso
movie	la película
movie star	la estrella de cine
moving	conmovedor, conmovedora
Oscar	el óscar
plot	el argumento; la trama
premiere	el estreno
rehearsal	el ensayo
to rehearse	ensayar
role	el papel
scene	la escena
screen	la pantalla
script	el guión
seat	la butaca
show	el show
stage	el escenario
subtitle	el subtítulo
success	el éxito
theater	el teatro
ticket	el tique
usher	el acomodador, la acomodadora

La música y la danza

El cine, la televisión y el teatro

Other arts: visual arts and materials

art gallery	la galería de arte
bust	el busto
canvas	el lienzo
caricature	la caricatura
ceramic, ceramics	la cerámica
contemporary	contemporáneo, -a
exhibit (noun)	la exposición
to exhibit	exponer
museum	el museo
to paint	pintar
painting	el cuadro
portrait	el retrato
sculpture	la escultura
statue	la estatua
studio	el taller
style	el estilo
watercolor	la acuarela

Hobbies

board	el tablero
card game	el juego de cartas
casino	el casino
checkers	las damas
chess	el ajedrez
chessboard	el tablero de ajedrez
to collect	coleccionar
collection	la colección
comic collection	la colección de los cómics
crossword puzzle	el crucigrama
festival	el festival
to fish	pescar
hobby	el hobby; el pasatiempo
wine tasting	la degustación

Literature

detective novel	la novela policíaca
fable	la fábula
fiction	la ficción
horror novel	la novela de horror
legend	la leyenda
literary work	la obra literaria
novelist	el/la novelista
paperback	la edición de bolsillo
poetry	la poesía
short story	el cuento

Physical activity, sports, and equipment	La actividad física, los deportes y el equipo
aerobics	el aeróbic
body building	el culturismo
to bowl	jugar a los bolos
bowling alley	la bolera
climbing	el alpinismo; el montañismo
endurance	la resistencia
exercise (noun)	el ejercicio
to exercise	hacer ejercicio
gym	el gimnasio
gymnastics	la gimnasia
hiker	el/la excursionista
hiking	la excursión
horseback riding	la equitación
to ice-skate	patinar sobre hielo
ice-skating	el patinaje sobre hielo
jogging	hacer jogging; el jogging
mat	la colchoneta
outdoor sports	los deportes al aire libre
pool	la piscina
roller skate	el patín de ruedas
to run	correr
ski (noun)	el esquí
to ski	esquiar
sneakers	las zapatillas de deporte
track	la pista de atletismo
to train	entrenar; entrenarse
yoga	el yoga

Team sports	Los deportes en equipo
American football	el fútbol americano
ball	la pelota
baseball	el béisbol
bat (noun)	el bate
to bat	batear
goal	el gol
goalkeeper	el portero, la portera
golf course	el campo de golfo
handball	el balonmano
to kick	patear
player	el jugador, la jugadora
to score	marcar un punto
scoreboard	el indicador
soccer	el fútbol
team	el equipo
tennis court	la cancha de tenis
to throw	lanzar
to tie	empatar
tied	empatado, -a
whistle (noun)	el silbato
to whistle	silbar

The sea and the beach

boat
to dive
to float
jet ski
kayak
to row
sailboat
sailing
submarine
sunburn
sunscreen moisturizer
to swim
swimming
water ski
to water-ski
wave
to windsurf

Camping

backpack
battery
cabin
to camp
camper
campfire
candle
fire
to go camping
hammock
inflatable bed
mosquito net
outdoors
picnic basket
sleeping bag
suntan lotion
water bottle

Eating out

bar
Bon appétit!
cordial
hors d'oeuvre
house specialty
to order
reservation
roast
roasted chicken
side dish
special
specialty

El mar y la playa

el bote
bucear
flotar
el jet
el kayak
remar
el velero
la vela
el submarino
la quemadura de sol
la crema con filtro solar
nadar
la natación
el esquí acuático
esquiar en el agua
la ola
hacer windsurf

El camping

la mochila
la pila
la cabaña
acampar
el/la campista
la fogata
la vela
el fuego
hacer camping
la hamaca
la cama hinchable
el mosquitero
al aire libre
la canasta de picnic
el saco de dormir
el bronceador
la cantimplora

Comer fuera de casa

el bar; la barra
¡Buen provecho!
el licor
el entremés; la tapa
la especialidad de la casa
pedir
la reserva
el asado
el pollo asado
la ración
el menú del día
la especialidad

Cognados. *Translate these words from English into Spanish; include the articles **el**, **la**, **los**, and **las** as necessary.*

1. orchestra (*f.*) _____

2. piano (*m.*) _____

3. flute (*f.*) _____

4. contemporary (*m.*) _____

5. jazz (*m.*) _____

6. rock (*m.*) _____

7. tango (*m.*) _____

8. rhythm (*m.*) _____

9. Cubism (*m.*) _____

10. museum (*m.*) _____

11. poem (*m.*) _____

12. judo (*m.*) _____

13. club (*m.*) _____

14. karate (*m.*) _____

15. ocean (*m.*) _____

16. autobiography (*f.*) _____

17. electric guitar (*f.*) _____

18. rugby (*m.*) _____

19. canoe (*f.*) _____

20. biography (*f.*) _____

21. photography (*f.*) _____

22. discotheque (*f.*) _____

23. horror novel (*f.*) _____

24. surfing (*m.*) _____

25. camping (*m.*) _____

26. sandwich (*m.*) _____

27. restaurant (*m.*) _____

28. tapa (*f.*) _____

29. menu (*m.*) _____

30. basketball (*m.*) _____

Palabras aprendidas en otros capítulos. *Translate these words from English into Spanish; include the articles **el, la, los,** and **las** as necessary.*

1. to cook _____
2. mobile home (*f.*) _____
3. tent (*f.*) _____
4. bike (*f.*) _____
5. salad (*f.*) _____
6. refreshment (*m.*) _____
7. barbecue (*f.*) _____
8. documentary (*m.*) _____
9. movie star (*f.*) _____
10. credit card (*f.*) _____
11. to float _____
12. beer (*f.*) _____
13. check (*f.*) _____
14. entrée (*m.*) _____
15. dessert (*m.*) _____
16. drink (*f.*) _____
17. dish (*m.*) _____
18. comedy (*f.*) _____
19. water (*m.*) _____
20. wine (*m.*) _____
21. to walk _____
22. to serve _____
23. ice cream parlor (*f.*) _____
24. lemonade (*f.*) _____
25. portion (*f.*) _____
26. price (*m.*) _____
27. spicy _____
28. tip (*f.*) _____
29. plan (*m.*) _____
30. to tip _____

JUEGO 10·3

Selección múltiple. *Choose the best ending for each sentence.*

1. Compramos en el cine dos tiques en ...
   a. el éxito.
   b. la taquilla.
   c. el escenario.
   d. la tienda de ropa.

2. Nos sentamos en el teatro en ...
   a. la hamaca.
   b. la casa móvil.
   c. la butaca.
   d. la tienda.

3. Esta obra es ridícula, horrible y el público quiere ...
   a. silbar.
   b. aplaudir.
   c. ensayar.
   d. pagar.

4. El público ríe porque la película es ...
   a. muy fea.
   b. un poco dramática.
   c. un poco limitada.
   d. muy cómica.

5. Este excelente actor recibió un óscar y significa ...
   a. el premio.
   b. el fracaso.
   c. la escena.
   d. la pantalla.

JUEGO 10·4

Traducción. *Try to guess what each phrase means and translate it into English.*

1. pasarlo bien _____

2. la broma _____

3. el parque de diversiones _____

4. la literatura infantil _____

5. los juegos de computadora _____

6. la tienda de los cómicos _____

7. dibujar _____

8. el juguete _____

9. la literatura juvenil _____

10. salir a bailar _____

11. el auditórium _____

12. tocar un instrumento _____

13. cantar _____

14. reír, reírse _____

15. el argumento; la trama _____

Un juego de palabras. *For each category below, choose the word or phrase that does not belong.*

1. **los niños se divierten con** la muñeca, el títere, la taquilla, el dibujo

2. **los actores necesitan** el ensayo, el papel, el acomodador, el teatro

3. **el camping** el submarino, la batería, el fuego, el mosquitero

4. **la comida fuera de casa** la reserva, el saco de dormir, la heladería, el menú

5. **la ropa para el ocio** el bañador, la gorra, las zapatillas, el esmoquin

6. **las actividades físicas** el aeróbic, la edición de bolsillo, la excursión, el patinaje

7. **la literatura** la batería, la leyenda, el cuento, el cuento de hadas

8. **la música** la canción, la voz, el coro, el lienzo

9. **las artes visuales** el busto, la cerámica, el casino, la exposición

10. **los deportes** el béisbol, la escultura, el fútbol, el balonmano

Palabras. *Fill in the letters needed to spell each Spanish word or phrase.*

1. __ n __ __ e __ e __ __ r __ e (*to amuse yourself*)

2. c __ __ t __ r r __ __ __ r (*to hum*)

3. d __ s __ __ n __ __ r (*to relax*)

4. __ e __ l __ __ a __ __ e (*to glide*)

5. m __ __ o __ __ __ í __ (*skateboard*)

6. __ i __ __ o __ u __ g __ (*video game*)

7. __ a __ l __ r (*to dance*)

8. c __ __ c __ ó __ (*song*)

9. __ r __ __ á __ __ __o (*dramatic*)

10. __ __ e __ __ o (*award*)

11. f __ a __ __ s __ (*flop*)

12. __ o __ m __ __e __ o __ (*moving*)

13. e __ __ r __ n __ (*premiere*)

14. __ s __ __ n __ r __ o (*stage*)

15. s __ b __ í __ __ l __ (*subtitle*)

Un juego acróstico. *Translate the clues on the left from English into Spanish. (You do not need to include articles.) Reading down the first letter of each word will then reveal a Spanish word.*

1. legend __ __ __ __ __ __

2. applause __ __ __ __ __ __ __

3. to throw __ __ __ __ __

4. scoreboard __ __ __ __ __ __ __ __

5. box office __ __ __ __ __ __ __

6. exciting __ __ __ __ __ __ __ __ __

7. to relax __ __ __ __ __ __ __ __

8. plot __ __ __ __ __ __ __

9. television __ __ __ __ __ __ __ __ __

10. to use __ __ __ __

11. endurance __ __ __ __ __ __ __ __ __ __

12. to camp __ __ __ __ __ __

La palabra vertical: _____

Palabras escondidas en este juego de puzle. *Find and circle the Spanish words hidden vertically, horizontally, and diagonally.*

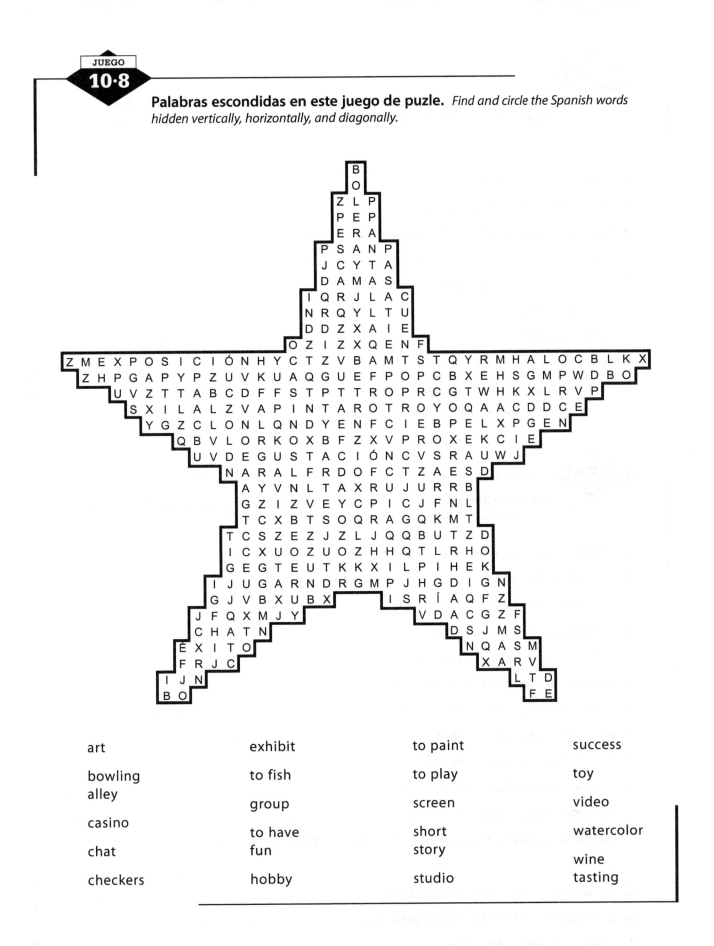

art	exhibit	to paint	success
bowling alley	to fish	to play	toy
casino	group	screen	video
chat	to have fun	short story	watercolor
checkers	hobby	studio	wine tasting

Adivinanza: el entretenimiento y más. *Guess what Spanish word or phrase corresponds to each definition or description.*

1. Para hacer las fotos. _____

2. Donde se ve la película. _____

3. Donde comprar los tiques para el concierto. _____

4. Para poder entender una película extranjera. _____

5. Para ver una exposición de cuadros. _____

6. Donde hay equipos para hacer ejercicios. _____

7. Para jugar tenis. _____

8. Donde jugar el golf. _____

9. Para llevar la ropa para un camping. _____

10. Para evitar la quemadura de sol. _____

Los deportes, las tiendas y más: juego de respuestas y preguntas. *Answers are given below. In English, write the corresponding questions.*

1. La colchoneta para el yoga, la gimnasia y más. _____.

2. Nadar para los deportes en la piscina. _____.

3. La persona que sube a la montaña. _____.

4. Deben ustedes ir a la gimnasia. _____.

5. Sí, tengo la dirección de la equitación. _____.

6. Aquí hay un lago pequeño para patinar. _____.

7. La tienda de deportes está cerca de aquí. _____.

8. Eso es deslizarse por un tobogán. _____.

9. A la derecha está la pista de atletismo. _____.

10. No, no me gustan los deportes al aire libre. _____.

11. Me dedico al montañismo. _____.

12. Mi hermana compra los pantalones pero no los patines de ruedas. _____.

13. Por supuesto, voy a correr con ustedes. _____.

14. Sí, el culturismo es muy esencial para mí. _____.

15. A veces yo juego a los bolos. _____.

El tiempo libre. *For each leisure activity, circle the letter of the item that belongs with it; then write out the answer in Spanish.*

1. Para pintar   a. el piano   b. el juego   c. la novela   d. el retrato

2. Para remar   a. el chiste   b. el bote   c. el festival   d. el avión

3. Para batear   a. la cantimplora   b. la fábula   c. el velero   d. el bate

4. Para esquiar   a. el bronceador   b. los poemas   c. los empates   d. el Internet

5. Para nadar   a. la caricatura   b. el bañador   c. la mochila   d. el pincel

6. Para jugar al ajedrez   a. el tablero   b. la poesía   c. el empatado   d. el silbato

7. Para bucear   a. la poesía   b. la campista   c. la vela   d. la piscina

8. Para ganar al golf   a. marcar puntos   b. patear   c. bucear   d. nadar

9. Para tocar música   a. la guitarra   b. los kayaks   c. los empates   d. la ola

10. Para entrenar   a. los deportes   b. los estilos   c. las cabañas   d. las fogatas

Crucigrama. *Fill in the crossword puzzle with the Spanish words or phrases.*

Horizontales (*Across*)

4. script
5. doll
7. puzzle
9. premiere
11. to visit

12. caricature
14. leisure
15. fiction
18. to hum
20. rehearsal

21. laughter
22. canvas
23. voice

Verticales (*Down*)

1. joke
2. puppet
3. ending
6. to collect

8. statue
10. to have fun
13. usher (*m.*)
16. group

17. backpack
19. reservation

La educación

Education

VOCABULARIO

Early childhood education

arts and crafts
to count
crayon
to draw
grade
grammar
kindergarten

number
to read
reading
school
to spell
spelling
writing

La educación primaria

las artes manuales
contar
el creyón
dibujar
el grado
la gramática
el kindergarten;
   el kinder
el número
leer
la lectura
la escuela; el colegio
deletrear
la ortografía
la escritura

Middle school and high school

algebra
anatomy
biology
calculus
chemistry
geography
geometry
history
literature
mathematics
music
physics
psychology
science
social science
space science
trigonometry
world languages

La educación secundaria

el álgebra
la anatomía
la biología
el cálculo
la química
la geografía
la geometría
la historia
la literatura
las matemáticas
la música
la física
la psicología, sicología
la ciencia
las ciencias sociales
las ciencias del espacio
la trigonometría
las lenguas extranjeras

Procedures and equipment

to attend
attendance
bell
blackboard

Los procedimientos y el equipo

asistir
la asistencia
la campana
la pizarra; el pizarrón

Procedures and equipment (cont.)

chalk	la tiza
classroom	el aula
computer lab	el laboratorio de computadoras
course	el curso
digital projector	el proyector digital
eraser	el borrador
graduation	la graduación
library	la biblioteca
projector	el proyector
recess	el recreo
schedule	el horario
scholarship	la beca
student	el/la estudiante
student desk	el pupitre
subject	la materia
substitute	el sustituto, la sustituta
to teach	dar clases; enseñar
teacher's desk	el escritorio del maestro

Class activities

to answer	responder
to ask	preguntar
to copy	copiar
to correct	corregir
debate	el debate
discussion	la discusión
essay	el ensayo
to explain	explicar
group work	el trabajo en equipo
homework	la tarea; el deber
to improve	mejorar
instruction	la instrucción
to learn	aprender
lecture	la conferencia
to obey	obedecer
to participate	participar
to take notes	tomar notas
to underscore	subrayar
to understand	entender
vacation	las vacaciones

Exams and grades

aptitude	la habilidad
to assess	evaluar
average	el promedio
difficult	difícil
diploma	el diploma
easy	fácil
exam	el examen
gifted	dotado, -a
to grade	calificar
mistake	el error
outstanding	excelente

Los procedimientos y el equipo (cont.)

Las actividades escolares

Los exámenes y las notas

Exams and grades (cont.)

pass [as a grade]; approved	aprobado
quiz	la prueba
to take an exam	tomar un examen

School supplies and materials

backpack	la mochila
binder	la carpeta
book	el libro
dictionary	el diccionario
to erase	borrar
eraser	el borrador; la goma de borrar
highlighter	el resaltador
marker	el marcador
notebook	el cuaderno
pen	el bolígrafo
pencil	el lápiz
pencil sharpener	el sacapuntas
ruler	la regla
sheet of paper	la hoja de papel
workbook	el cuaderno

Vocational training

audiovisual	audiovisual
audiovisual technology	los servicios audiovisuales
beauty school	la estética y peluquería
culinary school	la escuela culinaria
design (noun)	el diseño de modas
to design	diseñar
hospitality school	la escuela de hostelería
secretarial course	el secretariado
technology	la tecnología
therapy	la terapia

Higher education

to admit	ingresar
career	la carrera
college	la universidad
course credit	el crédito universitario
degree	el título
dissertation	la disertación
enrollment	la inscripción
faculty	la facultad
graduate (noun)	el graduado, la graduada
to graduate	graduar
master's degree	el título de máster
professor	el profesor, la profesora
to register	matricularse
registration	la matrícula
research (noun)	la investigación
to research	investigar
semester	semestre
seminar	el seminario
university	la universidad

Los exámenes y las notas (cont.)

Los útiles y materiales escolares

La formación profesional

La educación universitaria

Higher education schools and fields

accounting	la contabilidad
advertising	la publicidad
humanities	las humanidades
school of architecture	la escuela de arquitectura
school of education	la escuela de pedagogía
school of engineering	la escuela de ingeniería
school of journalism	la escuela de periodismo
school of law	la facultad de derecho
school of medicine	la facultad de medicina
school of pharmacy	la escuela de farmacia

Las facultades y las carreras universitarias

Computers and hardware

CD	el CD, los CD
CD-ROM	el CD-ROM
crash	bloquear
disk drive	el lector de discos
earphone	auricular
to install	instalar
key	la tecla
laptop	el ordenador portátil
memory	la memoria
modem	el módem
mouse	el ratón
to print	imprimir
printer	la impresora
to scan	escanear
scanner	el escáner
screen	la pantalla

Las computadoras y el hardware

Computer software

anti-virus software	el programa antivirus
click (noun)	el clic
to click	hacer clic
data bank	el banco de datos
to download	cargar
to highlight	resaltar
programmer	el programador
software package	el paquete de software
word processing	el procesamiento de textos

El software

Distance learning

fee	el pago de la matrícula
interactive	interactivo, -a
interactive exercises	los ejercicios interactivos
multimedia	multimedia
online class	la clase en línea
principal	el director, la directora
site	el sitio
teacher	el maestro, la maestra
user	el usuario, la usuaria
video camera	la videocámara
videoconference	la videoconferencia

Los cursos en línea

Cognados. *Translate these words from English into Spanish; include the articles **el, la, los**, and **las** as necessary.*

1. grade (*m.*) _____

2. grammar (*f.*) _____

3. vocabulary (*m.*) _____

4. biology (*f.*) _____

5. calculus (*m.*) _____

6. composition (*f.*) _____

7. history (*f.*) _____

8. music (*f.*) _____

9. to participate _____

10. laptop (*m.*) _____

11. click (*m.*) _____

12. exam (*m.*) _____

13. audiovisual _____

14. master (*m.*) _____

15. anatomy _____

16. kindergarten (*m.*) _____

17. class (*f.*) _____

18. semester (*m.*) _____

19. dictionary (*m.*) _____

20. university (*f.*) _____

21. multimedia (*f.*) _____

22. diploma (*m.*) _____

23. microphone (*m.*) _____

24. programmer (*m.*) _____

25. geography (*f.*) _____

26. mathematics (*f.*) _____

27. psychology (*f.*) _____

28. trigonometry (*f.*) _____

29. computer lab (*m.*) _____

30. telecommunication (*f.*) _____

Palabras aprendidas en otros capítulos. *Translate these words from English into Spanish; include the articles* **el, la, los,** *and* **las** *as necessary.*

1. art (*m.*) _____

2. book (*m.*) _____

3. to use _____

4. literature (*f.*) _____

5. to load _____

6. monitor (*m.*) _____

7. mouse (*m.*) _____

8. number (*m.*) _____

9. to participate _____

10. to print _____

11. to draw _____

12. ceramics (*f.*) _____

13. map (*m.*) _____

14. printer (*f.*) _____

15. program (*m.*) _____

16. reading (*f.*) _____

17. to scan _____

18. scanner (*m.*) _____

19. school (*f.*) _____

20. scissors (*f.*) _____

21. screen (*f.*) _____

22. vacation (*f.*) _____

23. to write _____

24. essay (*m.*) _____

25. keyboard (*m.*) _____

26. digital _____

En la escuela. *Circle the letter corresponding to the Spanish equivalent of each English word; then write the answer in Spanish.*

1. *to teach*   a. enseñar   b. comer   c. dibujar   d. preguntar

_____

2. *to spell*   a. contar   b. diseñar   c. escribir   d. deletrear

_____

3. *scholarship*   a. el escolar   b. el creyón   c. la beca   d. la tarea

_____

4. *principal*   a. el bolígrafo   b. el director   c. el proyector   d. el pupitre

_____

5. *attendance*   a. la pizarra   b. la tiza   c. la sustituta   d. la asistencia

_____

6. *schedule*   a. el horario   b. el recreo   c. el semestre   d. el lápiz

_____

7. *subject*   a. la materia   b. el material   c. el salón   d. la universidad

_____

8. *reading*   a. el arte   b. la lectura   c. la ortografía   d. el vocabulario

_____

9. *library*   a. el librero   b. la librería   c. la biblioteca   d. la libertad

_____

10. *site*   a. la clase   b. la usuaria   c. el sitio   d. el título

_____

Selección múltiple. *Choose the best completion for each statement below.*

1. Estudio en casa con ...
   a. los cursos en línea.
   b. el banco de datos.
   c. la educación primaria.
   d. las bibliotecas públicas.

2. En la escuela nos sentamos en ...
   a. la materia.
   b. el pupitre.
   c. el grado.
   d. la conferencia.

3. El maestro recoge los exámenes y va a …
   a. bloquear.
   b. instalar.
   c. ensayar.
   d. evaluar.

4. La formación profesional incluye …
   a. la arquitectura.
   b. la medicina.
   c. la estética y peluquería.
   d. la biología y la química.

5. Los procedimientos de clase incluyen …
   a. el premio.
   b. el seminario.
   c. la universidad.
   d. la ventana.

JUEGO 11·5

Los materiales escolares y los útiles: Adivinanza. *Guess what Spanish word or phrase corresponds to each definition or description.*

1. Para borrar las palabras en un papel. _____

2. Podemos recoger y devolver los libros aquí. _____

3. Cuando tres o más estudiantes trabajan juntos en la clase. _____

4. Para llevar los cuadernos y los libros a la clase. _____

5. Para encontrar las definiciones de las palabras. _____

6. Para escribir notas en la escuela. _____

7. Para sacar la punta de los lápices. _____

8. Para resaltar unas palabras en la página de un libro. _____

9. Para imprimir una página de la Web. _____

10. Para evitar un virus en la computadora. _____

JUEGO 11·6

Un juego de palabras. *For each category below, choose the word or phrase that does not belong.*

1. **los estudiantes traen a la clase** la mochila, el títere, la tarea, el libro

2. **las computadoras necesitan** el módem, la impresora, el ratón, la mochila

3. **en la educación secundaria aprenden** el cálculo, la química, la disertación, el álgebra

4. **los cursos en línea** la biblioteca, el sitio, los ejercicios interactivos, la videocámara

5. **los procedimientos en clase** la campana, la gorra, el proyector, el borrador

6. **las actividades escolares** la redacción, el ejercicio, la instrucción, el diploma

7. **los útiles en la clase** la carpeta, el sacapuntas, el cuento de hadas, el bolígrafo

8. **la formación profesional** la peluquería, la publicidad, la culinaria, la hostelería

9. **la educación universitaria** el secretariado, la inscripción, la matrícula, el seminario

10. **las notas del examen** aprobado, excelente, multimedia, reprobado

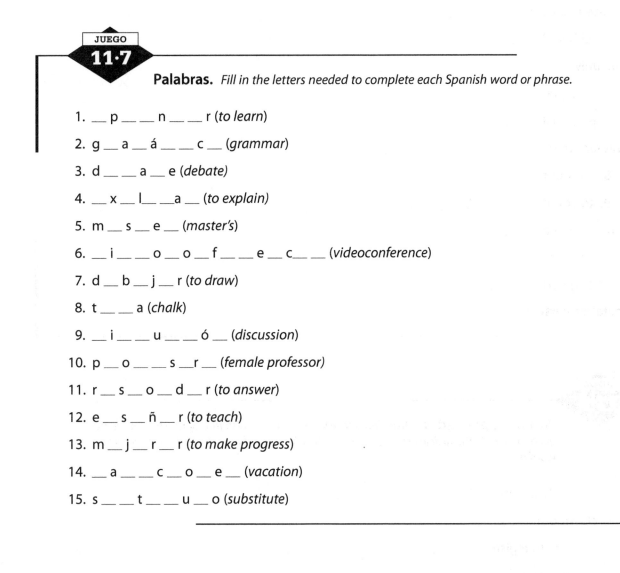

JUEGO

11·7

Palabras. *Fill in the letters needed to complete each Spanish word or phrase.*

1. __ p __ __ n __ __ r (*to learn*)

2. g __ a __ á __ __ c __ (*grammar*)

3. d __ __ a __ e (*debate*)

4. __ x __ l__ __a __ (*to explain*)

5. m __ s __ e __ (*master's*)

6. __ i __ __ o __ o __ f __ __ e __ c__ __ (*videoconference*)

7. d __ b __ j __ r (*to draw*)

8. t __ __ a (*chalk*)

9. __ i __ __ u __ __ ó __ (*discussion*)

10. p __ o __ __ s __r __ (*female professor*)

11. r __ s __ o __ d __ r (*to answer*)

12. e __ s __ ñ __ r (*to teach*)

13. m __ j __ r __ r (*to make progress*)

14. __ a __ __ c __ o __ e __ (*vacation*)

15. s __ __ t __ __ u __ o (*substitute*)

Un juego acróstico. *Translate the clues on the left from English into Spanish. (You do not need to include the articles.) Reading down the first letter of each word will then reveal a Spanish word or phrase.*

1. literature ▦ __ __ __ __ __ __ __ __ __
2. attendance ▦ __ __ __ __ __ __ __ __ __
3. blackboard ▦ __ __ __ __ __ __
4. university ▦ __ __ __ __ __ __ __ __ __
5. pen ▦ __ __ __ __ __ __ __
6. pencil ▦ __ __ __ __
7. interactive (f.) ▦ __ __ __ __ __ __ __ __ __
8. to count ▦ __ __ __ __ __
9. to admit ▦ __ __ __ __ __ __ __
10. diploma ▦ __ __ __ __ __ __
11. pass ▦ __ __ __ __ __ __
12. gifted ▦ __ __ __ __ __

La palabra vertical: _____

Palabras aprendidas. *Translate these words from English into Spanish. (You do not need to include the articles.) Reading down the highlighted letters will then reveal a Spanish word or phrase.*

1. literature ▦ __ __ __ __ __ __ __ __ __
2. classroom __ __ __ ▦
3. to register ▦ __ __ __ __ __ __ __ __ __ __ __
4. aptitude __ ▦ __ __ __ __ __ __
5. to understand __ __ ▦ __ __ __ __ __
6. printer __ __ __ __ ▦ __ __ __
7. average __ ▦ __ __ __ __ __
8. to grade __ __ __ __ ▦ __ __ __
9. screen __ ▦ __ __ __ __ __

La palabra vertical: _____

Palabras escondidas en este juego de puzle. *Find and circle the Spanish words hidden vertically, horizontally, and diagonally.*

```
O  R  T  O  G  R  A  F  Í  A  Y  G  J  D  F
Q  U  R  A  I  C  A  H  P  E  U  X  M  K  Q
N  F  W  D  F  U  M  T  E  Q  M  D  T  I  O
W  A  U  R  I  C  U  L  A  R  U  B  E  W  S
O  I  L  F  H  V  S  L  E  E  R  K  C  M  U
X  P  L  Y  T  M  E  R  Q  H  B  O  L  L  R
M  M  N  I  K  J  I  R  O  D  I  S  A  O  O
R  E  S  A  L  T  A  D  O  R  M  O  D  M  X
R  P  Z  U  S  E  S  V  A  U  I  A  O  A  C
D  W  W  I  U  M  J  R  S  R  R  U  I  T  I
R  L  S  Q  M  U  O  Y  A  R  I  R  S  E  E
O  A  O  K  Ó  H  W  U  O  A  O  N  J  R  N
S  L  P  Z  D  B  S  B  A  M  O  J  G  I  C
B  T  N  K  E  U  H  D  E  H  N  F  X  A  I
A  Q  C  J  M  J  Y  M  P  B  C  E  A  Z  A
```

to attend	highlighter	to read	subject
to crash	key	schedule	user
earphone	memory	science	
eraser	modem	spelling	

Crucigrama. *Fill in the crossword puzzle with the Spanish words.*

Horizontales (*Across*)

1. to copy
4. to obey
5. to learn
7. to spell
10. physics
13. bell
14. homework
15. to underscore
17. library
19. teacher (*m.*)

Verticales (*Down*)

1. conference
2. to highlight
3. graduation
6. mistake
8. difficult
9. mathematics
11. semester
12. education
16. scholarship
18. to read

Las materias y las carreras: Palabras escondidas en este juego de puzle. *Find and circle the Spanish words hidden vertically, horizontally, and diagonally.*

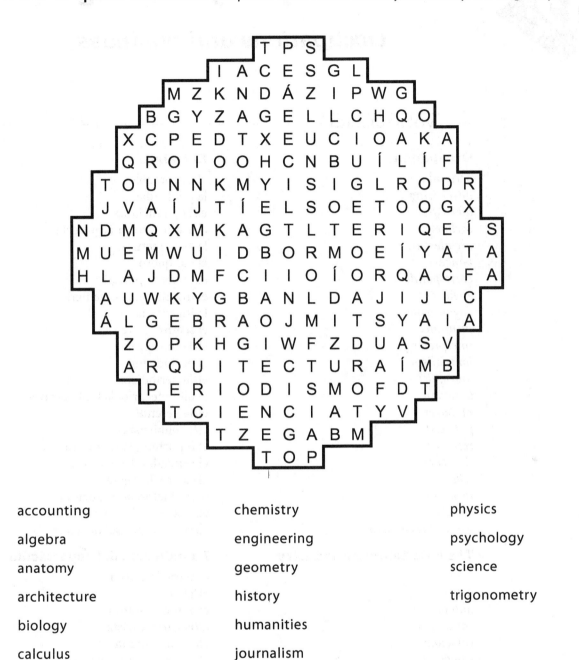

						T	P	S							
					I	A	C	E	S	G	L				
				M	Z	K	N	D	Á	Z	I	P	W	G	
			B	G	Y	Z	A	G	E	L	L	C	H	Q	O
		X	C	P	E	D	T	X	E	U	C	I	O	A	K	A
	Q	R	O	I	O	O	H	C	N	B	U	Í	L	Í	F
T	O	U	N	N	K	M	Y	I	S	I	G	L	R	O	D	R
J	V	A	Í	J	T	Í	E	L	S	O	E	T	O	O	G	X
N	D	M	Q	X	M	K	A	G	T	L	T	E	R	I	Q	E	Í	S
M	U	E	M	W	U	I	D	B	O	R	M	O	E	Í	Y	A	T	A
H	L	A	J	D	M	F	C	I	I	O	Í	O	R	Q	A	C	F	A
A	U	W	K	Y	G	B	A	N	L	D	A	J	I	J	L	C
Á	L	G	E	B	R	A	O	J	M	I	T	S	Y	A	I	A
Z	O	P	K	H	G	I	W	F	Z	D	U	A	S	V
A	R	Q	U	I	T	E	C	T	U	R	A	Í	M	B
P	E	R	I	O	D	I	S	M	O	F	D	T
T	C	I	E	N	C	I	A	T	Y	V
T	Z	E	G	A	B	M
T	O	P	

accounting	chemistry	physics
algebra	engineering	psychology
anatomy	geometry	science
architecture	history	trigonometry
biology	humanities	
calculus	journalism	

Los trabajos y el negocio

Occupations and business

Occupation — El trabajo

Occupation	El trabajo
accountant	el/la contable
advertising	la publicidad
advertiser	el/la anunciante
architect	el arquitecto, la arquitecta
architecture	la arquitectura
banker	el banquero
correspondent	el/la corresponsal
engineer	el ingeniero, la ingeniera
engineering	la ingeniería
insurance	el seguro
interpreter	el/la intérprete
journalism	el periodismo
journalist	el/la periodista
librarian	el bibliotecario, la bibliotecaria
manager	el/la gerente
publicist	el/la publicista
reporter	el reportero, la reportera
salesperson	el vendedor, la vendedora
teller	el cajero, la cajera
translator	el traductor, la traductora
travel agent	el/la agente de viajes
war correspondent	el/la corresponsal de guerra

The entertainment industry — La industria del espectáculo

The entertainment industry	La industria del espectáculo
actor	el actor, la actora
artist	el/la artista
author	el autor, la autora
cartoonist	el/la caricaturista
comedian	el/la comediante
composer	el compositor, la compositora
conductor	el director, la directora de orquesta
dancer	el bailarín, la bailarina
editor	el editor, la editora
film maker	el filmador, la filmadora
musician	el músico
playwright	el dramaturgo, la dramaturga
sculptor	el escultor, la escultora
singer	el/la cantante
writer	el escritor, la escritora

Health

anesthetist	el/la anestesista
cardiologist	el cardiólogo, la cardióloga
cosmetic surgery	la cirugía cosmética
dentist	el/la dentista
hygienist	el/la higienista
neurosurgeon	el neurocirujano, la neurocirujana
nurse	el enfermero, la enfermera
obstetrician	el/la obstetra
oncologist	el oncólogo, la oncóloga
ophthalmologist	el oftalmólogo, la oftalmóloga
pediatrician	el/la pediatra
plastic surgeon	el cirujano, la cirujana plástica
psychiatrist	el/la siquiatra
urologist	el urólogo, la uróloga
veterinarian	el veterinario, la veterinaria
X-ray technician	el técnico, la técnica de radiografía

La salud

Trades

apprentice	el aprendiz, la aprendiza
baker	el panadero, la panadera
bricklayer	el albañil
butcher	el carnicero, la carnicera
carpenter	el carpintero, la carpintera
chef	el/la chef
cook	el cocinero, la cocinera
driver	el/la chófer
electrician	el/la electricista
gardener	el jardinero, la jardinera
gardening	la jardinería
hairdresser	el peluquero, la peluquera
jeweler	el joyero, la joyera
license	la licencia
mechanic	el mecánico, la mecánica
occupation	la ocupación
painter	el pintor, la pintora
photographer	el fotógrafo, la fotógrafa
plumber	el fontanero, la fontanera
server	el camarero, la camarera
shoemaker	el zapatero, la zapatera
tailor	el/la sastre
technician	el técnico, la técnica
trade	el oficio; la ocupación
to train	entrenarse
training	la formación
waiter	el camarero
waitress	la camarera
watchmaker	el relojero, la relojera
worker	el obrero, la obrera

Los oficios

The bank

account	la cuenta
automated teller machine (ATM)	el cajero automático
balance	el saldo
checking account	la cuenta corriente
deposit (noun)	el depósito
to deposit	depositar
to fill out	rellenar
loan	el préstamo
password	la clave; la contraseña
to save	ahorrar
savings account	la cuenta de ahorro
statement	el estado de cuentas
window	la ventanilla
to withdraw	sacar dinero

El banco

Looking for a job

to apply for a job	solicitar empleo
appointment	la cita
candidate	el candidato, la candidata
company	la empresa
employee	el empleado, la empleada
to hire	emplear
interview	la entrevista
job	el empleo
job application	la solicitud de empleo
vacancy	la plaza vacante

En busca de empleo

Labor-management relations

agreement	el acuerdo
boycott (noun)	el boicot
to boycott	boicotear
to fire someone	despedir a alguien
judge	el juez, la jueza
lawyer	el abogado, la abogada
layoff	el despido
to negotiate	negociar
negotiation	la negociación
to protest	protestar
strike	la huelga
striker	el/la huelguista
union	el sindicato

Las relaciones entre el trabajador y la empresa

Rights, compensation, and benefits

holiday	el día feriado
pay raise	el aumento de sueldo
pension	la pensión; el retiro
promotion	el ascenso
resignation	la renuncia
salary, wage	el salario; el sueldo
Social Security	la seguridad social
unemployment insurance	el seguro de desempleo
vacation	las vacaciones

Los derechos, la compensación y los beneficios

Finance and the economy

auction	la subasta
audit	la auditoría
bankruptcy	la bancarrota
budget	el presupuesto
currency	la moneda
entrepreneur	el empresario, la empresaria
gain	la ganancia
investment	la inversión
investor	el/la inversionista
to liquidate	liquidar
loss	la pérdida
quote	el presupuesto
share	la acción de valor
shareholder	el/la accionista
speculator	el especulador, la especuladora
stock exchange	la bolsa de valores
takeover	la adquisición

Las finanzas y la economía

Professional sports

athletic	atlético, -a
athletics	el atletismo
automobile race	la carrera automovilística
ballplayer	el pelotero, la pelotera
basketball player	el jugador de basquetbol
biking	el ciclismo
car racing	la carrera de autos
champion	el campeón, la campeona
championship	el campeonato
cup	la copa
football player	el futbolista
goalkeeper	el portero, la portera
golfer	el/la golfista
hockey player	el jugador de hockey
professional athlete	el/la atleta profesional
to race	competir
racecar driver	el auto de carreras
soccer player	el jugador de fútbol
tennis player	el/la tenista
tournament	el torneo
trainer	el entrenador, la entrenadora
umpire	el árbitro, la árbitra
to win	ganar
winner	el ganador, la ganadora

Los deportes profesionales

Cognados. *Translate these words from English into Spanish; include the articles **el**, **la**, **los**, and **las** as necessary.*

1. tourist (*m./f.*) _____

2. agenda (*f.*) _____

3. contract (*m.*) _____

4. sector (*m.*) _____

5. visa (*f.*) _____

6. jet (*m.*) _____

7. security (*f.*) _____

8. association (*f.*) _____

9. dentist (*m./f.*) _____

10. pharmacist (*m./f.*) _____

11. to protest _____

12. veterinarian (*m.*) _____

13. to practice _____

14. engineering (*f.*) _____

15. reporter (*f.*) _____

16. golf (*m.*) _____

17. pilot (*m./f.*) _____

18. corporation (*f.*) _____

19. solution (*f.*) _____

20. protest (*f.*) _____

21. record (*m.*) _____

22. compromise (*m.*) _____

23. experience (*f.*) _____

24. medical doctor (*m./f.*) _____

25. pension (*f.*) _____

26. candidate (*m.*) _____

27. artist (*m./f.*) _____

28. interest (*m.*) _____

29. speculator (*f.*) _____

30. athletic (*m./f.*) _____

Palabras aprendidas en otros capítulos. *Translate these words from English into Spanish; include the articles **el**, **la**, **los**, and **las** as necessary.*

1. to earn _____

2. emergency exit (*f.*) _____

3. to fasten _____

4. captain (*m.*) _____

5. exit (*f.*) _____

6. nurse (*m./f.*) _____

7. bank (*m.*) _____

8. work (*m.*) _____

9. police (*f.*) _____

10. surgeon (*m./f.*) _____

11. sculpture (*f.*) _____

12. library (*f.*) _____

13. to paint _____

14. psychologist (*f.*) _____

15. jewel (*f.*) _____

16. seat (*m.*) _____

17. seatbelt (*m.*) _____

18. speed (*f.*) _____

19. window (*f.*) _____

20. to park _____

21. anesthesiologist (m./f.) _____
22. electricity (f.) _____
23. to dance _____
24. author (m./f.) _____
25. editor (m./f.) _____

26. travel agent (m./f.) _____
27. theater (m.) _____
28. loan (m.) _____
29. comedy (f.) _____
30. painting (f.) _____

JUEGO
12·3

Selección múltiple. *Choose the best completion for each statement.*

1. Tú trabajas en el teatro y ves ...
   a. el torneo.
   b. la inversionista.
   c. el escenario.
   d. la ingeniera.

2. Este joven aprende su trabajo porque es ...
   a. un cardiólogo.
   b. un contable.
   c. un periodista.
   d. un aprendiz.

3. Me encantan las novelas y ella es ...
   a. la escritora.
   b. la corresponsal de guerra.
   c. la cantante.
   d. la bailarina.

4. Mila pone las notas de música y es ...
   a. una filmadora.
   b. una panadera.
   c. una compositora.
   d. una fotógrafa.

5. Estos hombres trabajan en la orquesta:
   a. los zapateros.
   b. los músicos.
   c. los peluqueros.
   d. los electricistas.

JUEGO
12·4

Traducción. *Translate from Spanish into English.*

1. la cirugía cosmética _____
2. el desempleo _____
3. la plaza vacante _____
4. el día feriado _____
5. la carrera automovilística _____
6. el carnicero, la carnicera _____
7. la licencia _____
8. el/la accionista _____
9. el aumento de sueldo _____

10. el cocinero, la cocinera _____

11. la seguridad social _____

12. el/la chófer _____

JUEGO
12·5

Palabras. *Fill in the letters needed to complete each Spanish word or phrase.*

1. c _ _ _ e _ _o _ s _ _ (*correspondent*)

2. _ e_ _ r _ (*insurance*)

3. _ i _l _ _ t _ c _ _ _ o (*librarian*)

4. e _ _ u _ _ o _ (*sculptor*)

5. _a _ q _e _ o (*banker*)

6. _ d _ _ o _ a (*editor*)

7. m _ _ i _ o (*musician*)

8. _ a _ i _ _ t _ _ i _ t _ (*cartoonist*)

9. p _ d _ _ t_ a (*pediatrician*)

10. _ a _ a _ e _ o (*baker*)

11. j _ _ d _ n _ _ o (*gardener*)

12. _ e _ d _ _ _ o _ a (*salesperson*)

13. _ n _ é _ p _ _t _ (*interpreter*)

14. p _ b _ i _ _ d _ d (*advertisement*)

15. _ e _ _ o d _ _ _ o (*journalism*)

JUEGO
12·6

Un juego de palabras. *For each category below, choose the word or phrase that does not belong.*

1. **los reporteros están en** la conferencia, la oficina, la bancarrota, la calle

2. **las ocupaciones son** los ascensos, los bancos, los deportes profesionales, los teatros

3. **la educación universitaria se necesita para ser** ingeniero, intérprete, periodista, albañil

4. **las ocupaciones de la salud** la obstetra, el cirujano, el panadero, la cardióloga

5. **los procedimientos en la cirugía** el técnico de radiografía, la gorra de los enfermeros, la cirujana, el despido

6. **los oficios y las ocupaciones** el pintor, la fontanera, la escultora, el mecánico

7. **los bancos** la cuenta, el préstamo, la contraseña, el anestesista

8. **la formación profesional incluye** la jardinería, la publicidad, la culinaria, la hostelería

9. **los oficios incluyen** el chofer, la carpintera, el peluquero, el urólogo

10. **las finanzas** la auditoría, el empresario, el sindicato, la inversionista

JUEGO 12·7

Palabras escondidas en este juego de puzle. *Find and circle the Spanish equivalents of these words hidden vertically, horizontally, and diagonally.*

```
O A Q U T S S E Q P D C W E O I U
W X J S F P S I G E R E N T E K N
M U F W C S Q S J S A S T R E G W
R H L F L R R Z D M M N O Q F Z F
I I Y F W A N L C Y A C K Z U X C
E L E C T R I C I S T A E Y B M E
P S V E O H C R P M U S G E G T C
F O I J E N I O J W R E U I N C O
L Z R Q F K Q G C R G O H E E Q M
B L C T U I H U I F O Q G J I Y E
Á A O B E I L H E E K A T H F X D
K R N H L R A M C A N T A N T E I
U U B Q U I A T A J J I B B R O A
N S I I U J Y Z R D U D S O B W N
W M V R T E T Q Y A O E E T Y L T
G I S G E R R V D F V R Z V A H E
O F I C I O O O J K P A A B Z D Z
```

agent	goalkeeper (*f.*)	psychiatrist (*f.*)
banker (*m.*)	hygienist	singer
comedian (*f.*)	judge (*m.*)	tailor
electrician	manager	trade
film maker (*f.*)	playwright (*m.*)	umpire (*m.*)

La salud, la ganancia y otros: Adivinanza. *Guess what Spanish word or phrase corresponds to each definition or description.*

1. Para tratar el cáncer. _____

2. Para entender lo que hemos gastado en el banco. _____

_____

3. Para sacar el dinero fuera del banco. _____

4. Para entender lo que se dice en portugués, francés y otros idiomas. _____

_____

5. Para revisar la vista de los ojos. _____

6. Para ahorrar dinero en el banco. _____

7. Para revisar los dientes en la boca. _____

8. Para poder comprar un apartamento. _____

9. Para pedir el desayuno en el restaurante. _____

10. Para revisar el auto. _____

Los empleos. *Translate from English into Spanish; include the article **el**, **la**, **los**, or **las** as necessary.*

1. biking __ __   __ __ __ __ __ __ __ __

2. technician (*f.*) __ __   __ __ __ __ __ __ __ __

3. worker (*m.*) __ __   __ __ __ __ __ __ __

4. job __ __   __ __ __ __ __ __

5. champion (*m.*) __ __   __ __ __ __ __ __ __ __

6. watchmaker (*f.*) __ __   __ __ __ __ __ __ __ __

7. balance __ __   __ __ __ __ __ __

8. interview __ __   __ __ __ __ __ __ __ __ __

9. striker (*f.*) __ __   __ __ __ __ __ __ __ __ __

10. employee (*m.*) __ __   __ __ __ __ __ __ __ __

11. car racing __ __ __ __ __ __ __ __ __ __ __ __ __ __ __ __ __

12. checking account __ __ __ __ __ __ __ __ __ __ __ __ __ __ __ __

13. budget __ __ __ __ __ __ __ __ __ __ __ __ __

14. auction __ __ __ __ __ __ __ __ __

15. champion (f.) __ __ __ __ __ __ __ __ __ __ __

Un juego acróstico. *Translate the clues on the left from English into Spanish. (You do not need to include the articles.) Reading down the first letter of each word will then reveal a Spanish word or phrase.*

1. to liquidate ▧ __ __ __ __ __ __ __ __

2. agent ▧ __ __ __ __ __

3. musicians (m.) ▧ __ __ __ __ __ __ __

4. obstetrician (f.) ▧ __ __ __ __ __ __ __ __

5. neurosurgeon (m.) ▧ __ __ __ __ __ __ __ __ __ __ __ __ __ __

6. editor (f.) ▧ __ __ __ __ __ __ __

7. orchestra conductor (f.) ▧ __ __ __ __ __ __ __ __

8. architecture ▧ __ __ __ __ __ __ __ __ __ __ __

La palabra vertical: _____

Crucigrama. *Fill in the crossword puzzle with the Spanish words.*

Horizontales (*Across*)

2. resignation

6. appointment

7. gain

8. loss

10. manager (*m./f.*)

12. advertiser (*m./f.*)

13. to race

14. salary

15. account

16. shareholder (*f.*)

18. to deposit

Verticales (*Down*)

1. strike

3. winner (*f.*)

4. deposit

5. to train

6. championship

9. agreement

11. to hire

13. teller (*m.*)

14. insurance

17. cup

El gobierno, la sociedad y las relaciones internacionales

Government, society, and international relations

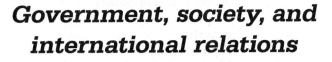

·13·

Government system

assembly
authority
congress
crown
deputy
dictatorship
executive power
fatherland
flag
to govern
government
governor
head of state
leader
legislature
minister (of government)
monarch
monarchy
national
patriotism
president
regime
secretary of state
senate
senator
state
vice-president

El sistema de gobierno

la asamblea
la autoridad
el congreso
la corona
el diputado, la diputada
la dictadura
el poder ejecutivo
la patria
la bandera
gobernar
el gobierno
el gobernador, la gobernadora
el/la jefe de estado
el/la líder
la legislatura
el ministro, la ministra
el/la monarca
la monarquía
nacional
el patriotismo
el presidente
el régimen
el secretario, la secretaria de estado
el senado
el senador, la senadora
el estado; la nación
el/la vicepresidente, la vicepresidenta

Elections, parties, and civil administration

to abstain
alliance
city hall
coalition
conservative
to count
democratic
to elect
independent
inspector

Las elecciones, los partidos y la administración pública

abstenerse
la alianza
el ayuntamiento
la coalición
conservador
contar; contar los votos
demócrata
elegir
independiente
el inspector, la inspectora

Elections, parties, and civil administration (cont.)

left	la izquierda
liberal	liberal
mayor	el alcalde
opponent	el opositor, la opositora
opposition	la oposición
party	el partido
politician	el político, la política
polling booth	la cabina de votación
presidential	presidencial
right	la derecha
tax	el impuesto, los impuestos
taxpayer	el/la contribuyente
term	el mandato
town hall	la alcaldía
vote (noun)	el voto
to vote	votar

Las elecciones, los partidos y la administración pública (cont.)

Rights and society

birthright	el derecho de nacimiento
citizen	el ciudadano, la ciudadana
citizenship	la ciudadanía
deportation	la deportación
discrimination	la discriminación
foreigner	el extranjero, la extranjera
green card	la tarjeta verde
identity	la identidad
illegal	ilegal
immigrant	el/la inmigrante
immigration	la inmigración
minority	la minoría
naturalization	la naturalización
permit (noun)	el permiso
to permit	permitir
prejudice	el prejuicio
right	el derecho
undocumented	indocumentado, -a

Los derechos y la sociedad

Law and justice

to accuse	acusar
accused	acusado, -a
to acquit	absolver
alleged	presunto, -a
to appeal	apelar
to blame	imputar
to condemn	condenar
convict	el convicto, la convicta
court	la corte
criminal court	el tribunal
death	la muerte
defense	la defensa
fingerprints	las huellas
guilt	la culpabilidad

La ley y la justicia

Law and justice (cont.)

guilty	culpable
innocence	la inocencia
to investigate	investigar
investigation	la investigación
jail	la cárcel
judge	el/la juez
jury	el jurado
lawyer	el abogado, la abogada
liberty	la libertad
life imprisonment	la cadena perpetua
notary	el notario, la notaria
oath	el juramento
to plead	declararse
police	la policía
policeman	el/la policía
police station	la estación de policía
prisoner	el prisionero, la prisionera
respect (noun)	el respeto
to respect	respetar
to sentence	sentenciar
to testify	testificar
trial	el juicio
witness	el/la testigo

La ley y la justicia (cont.)

Crime

blackmail	el chantaje
burglar	el ladrón, la ladrona
burglary	el robo
delinquency	la delincuencia
embezzlement	el desfalco
to falsify	falsificar
fire	el incendio
flame	la llama
forgery	la falsificación
fraud	el fraude
gangster	el gángster
homicide	el homicidio
kidnapper	el secuestrador, la secuestradora
kidnapping	el secuestro
to kill	asesinar; matar
murderer	el asesino, la asesina
to steal	robar
swindle	la estafa
thief	el ladrón, la ladrona
vandalism	el vandalismo
victim	la víctima

El crimen

International politics, war, and peace

ambassador	el embajador, la embajadora
armament	el armamento
arms	las armas
attack (noun)	el ataque

Las relaciones internacionales, la guerra y la paz

International politics, war, and peace (cont.)

to attack	atacar
civil war	la guerra civil
consul	el/la cónsul
consulate	el consulado
defeat	la derrota
deserter	el desertor, la desertora
diplomatic	diplomático, -a
diplomatic corps	el cuerpo diplomático
disarmament	el desarme
embassy	la embajada
hostility	la hostilidad
to lose	perder
NATO	la OTÁN
pacifism	el pacifismo
pacifist	el/la pacifista
pact	el pacto
peace	la paz
power	el poder
reconciliation, bringing together	el acercamiento
sanction	la sanción
to surrender	rendirse
treason	la traición
treaty	el tratado
ultimatum	el ultimátum
understanding	el acuerdo
United Nations	Organización de las Naciones Unidas
victory	la victoria
to wound	herir
wounded	el herido, la herida

Military forces and equipment / Las fuerzas armadas y el equipo

ambulance	la ambulancia
army	el ejército
artillery	la artillería
battalion	el batallón
bomb (noun)	la bomba
to bomb	bombardear
bombardment	el bombardeo
capture	la captura
to capture	capturar
commander in chief	el/la jefe de las fuerzas armadas
to destroy	destruir
division	la división
to explode	explotar
explosive	el explosivo
fear	el miedo, el terror
fire	el fuego
to fire	disparar
firefighter	el bombero, la bombera
general	el/la general
helicopter	el helicóptero
infantry	la infantería
intervention	la intervención

Military forces and equipment (cont.)	Las fuerzas armadas y el equipo (cont.)
medical equipment	el equipo médico
militia	la milicia
mine	la mina
navy	la marina
panic	el pánico
to ransack	saquear
revolver	el revólver
rifle	el rifle
sabotage	el sabotaje
security	la seguridad
soldier	el soldado
spy	el espía
submarine	el submarino
tank	el tanque
traumatic	traumático, -a
troop	la tropa

JUEGO

13·1

Cognados. *Translate these words from English into Spanish; include the articles **el**, **la**, **los**, and **las** as necessary.*

1. capitalism (m.) _____

2. republic (f.) _____

3. bureaucracy (f.) _____

4. nation (f.) _____

5. communist _____

6. democracy (f.) _____

7. region (f.) _____

8. origin (m.) _____

9. nation (f.) _____

10. socialist _____

11. to attack _____

12. liberty (f.) _____

13. sentence (f.) _____

14. minority (f.) _____

15. detective (m./f.) _____

16. constitution (f.) _____

17. discrimination (f.) _____

18. candidate (m./f.) _____

19. democratic (m./f.) _____

20. racism (m.) _____

21. immigrant (m./f.) _____

22. assembly (f.) _____

23. legal _____

24. intolerance (f.) _____

25. innocent _____

26. evidence (f.) _____

27. prison (f.) _____

28. testimony (m.) _____

29. verdict (m.) _____

30. sanction (f.) _____

¿Verdadero o falso? *True or false? Write V (for **verdad**/true) or F (for **falso**/false) next to each sentence.*

1. _____ La defensa tiene que ver con la ley y la justicia.

2. _____ La crisis tiene que ver con la economía y las guerras.

3. _____ El rey es el jefe de estado de los Estados Unidos.

4. _____ Los ciudadanos de los Estados Unidos pueden votar a los dieciocho años.

5. _____ El congreso de los Estados Unidos elige el gabinete del presidente en los Estados Unidos.

6. _____ Tenemos 100 senadores en los Estados Unidos.

7. _____ En Estados Unidos los votantes eligen al secretario / a la secretaria de estado.

8. _____ La ideología del partido comunista se considera de derecha.

9. _____ España es solamente una monarquía.

10. _____ En los Estados Unidos elegimos un presidente cada seis años.

Selección múltiple. *Choose the best completion for each sentence.*

1. En Washington en los Estados Unidos tenemos ...
   a. una monarquía.
   b. un sistema comunista.
   c. un presidente elegido.
   d. una dictadora.

2. En las ciudades pequeñas hay ...
   a. un alcalde.
   b. un cuerpo diplomático.
   c. un jefe de estado.
   d. un consulado.

3. Los ciudadanos pueden votar en ...
   a. el derecho de nacimiento.
   b. el juicio.
   c. la cabina de votación.
   d. la estación de policía.

4. El crimen es ...
   a. patriotismo.
   b. investigar.
   c. elegir.
   d. robar.

5. Las relaciones internacionales tienen que ver con ...
   a. los jurados.
   b. las falsificaciones.
   c. el vandalismo.
   d. la diplomacia.

Las elecciones, el crimen y más. *Translate from English into Spanish; include the article **el**, **la**, **los**, or **las** as necessary.*

1. thief __ __ __ __ __ __ __ __

2. kidnapping __ __ __ __ __ __ __ __ __ __ __

3. victim __ __ __ __ __ __ __ __

4. vandalism __ __ __ __ __ __ __ __ __ __ __

5. murderer (*f.*) __ __ __ __ __ __ __ __ __

6. to falsify __ __ __ __ __ __ __ __ __ __

7. embezzlement __ __ __ __ __ __ __ __ __

8. intervention __ __ __ __ __ __ __ __ __ __ __ __

9. pact __ __ __ __ __ __

10. fraud __ __ __ __ __ __ __

11. gangster __ __ __ __ __ __ __ __ __

12. to kill __ __ __ __ __ __ __

13. homicide __ __ __ __ __ __ __ __ __

14. swindle __ __ __ __ __ __ __

15. witness (*m.*) __ __ __ __ __ __ __ __

16. authority __ __ __ __ __ __ __ __ __ __

17. dictatorship __ __ __ __ __ __ __ __ __

18. fatherland __ __ __ __ __ __ __

19. alliance __ __ __ __ __ __ __ __

20. to vote __ __ __ __ __

21. coalition __ __ __ __ __ __ __ __ __ __ __

Las relaciones internacionales: Adivinanza. *Guess what Spanish word or phrase corresponds to each definition or description.*

1. La persona que representa al estado en otras naciones. _____

2. Es un soldado que abandona su bandera y no ayuda a otros soldados. _____

_____

3. Las ideas para promover la paz entre muchas naciones. _____

4. Es una persona que protege las personas de su propia nación en países extranjeros.

_____

5. Es una idea para mantener la paz y no traer las armas entre muchas naciones. _____

_____

6. Las letras iniciales, como abreviaturas, de esta organización son ONU. _____

_____

7. El pueblo es armado para derrotar la dictadura. _____

8. La última solución que dan los diplomáticos para evitar la guerra.

_____

9. Esto significa arrojar bombas desde un avión. _____

10. Es un derecho internacional para resolver problemas de guerras entre muchos países.

_____

Un juego de palabras. *For each expression or category below, choose the word or phrase that does **not** belong.*

1. **los líderes de** los gobiernos, las comunidades, los deportes, las gorras

2. **las leyes vienen de** la legislatura, los convictos, el presidente, el senado

3. **el sistema de gobierno incluye** la gobernadora, la legislatura, el ladrón, el ayuntamiento

4. **la vicepresidente de** la compañía de negocios, los Estados Unidos, el comité de una universidad, la bandera

5. **los ciudadanos de los E.E.U.U. votan en** la alcaldía, la embajada, las Fuerzas Armadas, la muerte

6. **los voluntarios tienen miedo a** la iglesia, la estación de policía, el explosivo, el detective

7. **un uniforme es necesario para** un bombero, un policía, un soldado, un ilegal

8. **un símbolo de paz** la paloma blanca, la pistola negra, la bandera blanca, la bandera de la Cruz Roja

9. **necesitan un láptop** la estación de los bomberos, los albañiles, los periodistas, la alcaldía

10. **las ocupaciones de los gobiernos** el presidente, el gobernador, la senadora, la peluquería

Palabras escondidas en este juego de puzle. *Find and circle the Spanish words hidden vertically, horizontally, and diagonally.*

```
V M R C U K D K H U D N J O T J S Q K
V O F F U Y U K Y Q U W D D B Q T K U
I K Z D A N F R R M U E N D V E R F C
Z X C E V I C T O R I A O B D I E F M
S F W A O Y C L B M O R C Z H X X P G
M J J E B W R T Z G E O N X A N P Z J
Z Q J A X L W B E B B D H K L T L A Y
C U R N R O U M D M J L Q Z H O L A
I E S Y X D F O A Q L Z G O D M S B O
U I T I A U B L O X Y E X Q U O I W D
D Z O G M X S P S A D K Y D D Y V G Q
A X O K O R C H R I F P T R B N O W Y
D B Y U B P C W N E V E E X F T F T R
A X H P Q O A Y E I J U P G S E O A H
N O Q H W P M C Q S C U I Á C S L N E
A F U V T P L B U A W X I M N T J Q R
V K C C K R K T A S G P C C N I B U I
Z X V D E V M I A G A A O M I G C E R
A L C A L D E W D M X R P K N O Z O V
```

to accuse	firefighter (*m.*)	understanding
bomb	lawyer (*m.*)	victory
citizen (*f.*)	mayor	witness (*m.*)
explosive	panic	to wound
fear	prejudice	
fire	tank	

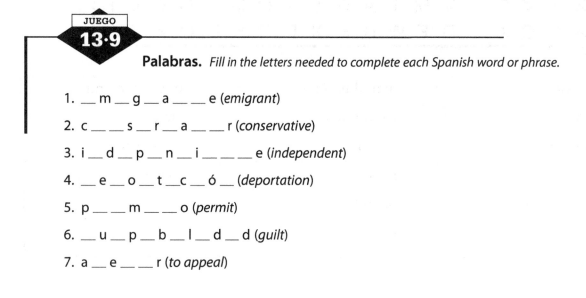

JUEGO 13·8

Un juego acróstico. *Translate the clues on the left from English into Spanish. (You do not need to include articles.) Reading down the first letter of each word will then reveal a Spanish word or phrase.*

1. to elect ▦ __ __ __ __ __
2. leader ▦ __ __ __ __
3. assembly ▦ __ __ __ __ __ __ __
4. life imprisonment ▦ __ __ __ __ __ __ __ __ __ __ __ __
5. army ▦ __ __ __ __ __ __
6. gun ▦ __ __ __ __ __ __ __
7. coalition ▦ __ __ __ __ __ __ __ __
8. authorities ▦ __ __ __ __ __ __ __ __ __ __
9. monarchy ▦ __ __ __ __ __ __ __ __
10. inspector ▦ __ __ __ __ __ __ __ __
11. explosive ▦ __ __ __ __ __ __ __
12. naturalization ▦ __ __ __ __ __ __ __ __ __ __ __ __ __
13. to testify ▦ __ __ __ __ __ __ __ __ __
14. opposition ▦ __ __ __ __ __ __ __ __

La palabra vertical: _____

JUEGO 13·9

Palabras. *Fill in the letters needed to complete each Spanish word or phrase.*

1. __ m __ g __ a __ __ e (*emigrant*)
2. c __ __ s __ r __ a __ __ r (*conservative*)
3. i __ d __ p __ n __ i __ __ __ e (*independent*)
4. __ e __ o __ t __ c __ ó __ (*deportation*)
5. p __ __ m __ __ o (*permit*)
6. __ u __ p __ b __ l __ d __ d (*guilt*)
7. a __ e __ __ r (*to appeal*)

8. __ n __ c __ n __ i __ (*innocence*)

9. __ e __ t __ n __ i __ r (*to sentence*)

10. __ n __ e __ d __ o (*fire*)

11. c __ a __ t __ __ e (*blackmail*)

12. __ __ t __ ll __ __ í __ (*artillery*)

13. e __ __ a __ a (*swindle*)

14. __ í __ t __ __ a (*victim*)

15. i __ f __ n __ e __ í __ (*infantry*)

Palabras aprendidas. *Translate these words from English into Spanish. (You do not need to include articles.) Reading down the boxed column will then reveal a Spanish word or phrase.*

1. foreigner (*f.*) 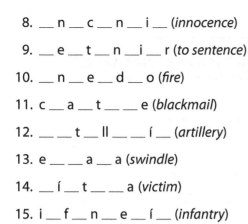 __ __ __ __ __ __ __ __ __

2. to acquit __ __ __ __ ▦ __ __ __

3. immigration ▦ __ __ __ __ __ __ __ __ __ __

4. minister (*m.*) ▦ __ __ __ __ __ __ __

5. guilty __ __ __ ▦ __ __ __

6. naturalization __ __ __ ▦ __ __ __ __ __ __ __ __

7. alleged __ __ ▦ __ __ __ __ __

8. fingerprints __ __ __ __ __ __ ▦

9. notary (*f.*) __ __ ▦ __ __ __ __

10. to condemn __ ▦ __ __ __ __ __ __

La palabra vertical: _____

La justicia, la guerra y más: Palabras revueltas o anagrama de este capítulo. *Unscramble each Spanish word below and write it out correctly.*

1. r / s / e / t / a / r / p / e _____

2. d / e / l / c / a / r / a / e / r / s _____

3. a / b / t / a / ó / ll / n _____

4. p / c / a / i / i / s / f / t / a _____

5. d / v / i / i / ó / s / i / n _____

6. d / s / e / t / i / r / u / r _____

7. a / m / r / a / m / n / e / t / o _____

8. o / p / d / r / e _____

9. t / r / i / a / c / ó / i / n _____

10. c / p / a / t / r / u / a / r _____

11. p / e / u / q / i / o   c / m / d / i / é / o (*2 words*) _____

12. s / b / a / o / a / t / e / j _____

13. s / a / u / q / e / r / a _____

14. d / s / i / p / r / a / r / a _____

15. m / r / a / n / a / i _____

Crucigrama. *Fill in the crossword puzzle with the words in Spanish.*

Horizontales (*Across*)

1. delinquency
5. to surrender
8. investigation

10. to abstain
12. to testify
15. to explode

16. traumatic
17. militia
18. fear

Verticales (*Down*)

2. taxpayer
3. hostility
4. security

6. oath
7. ultimatum
9. opponent (*f.*)

11. deputy (*m.*)
13. to blame
14. panic

El mundo y la naturaleza

The world and nature

Space	**El espacio**
air	el aire
astronaut	el/la astronauta
astronomy	la astronomía
atmosphere	la atmósfera
celestial body	el astro
comet	el cometa
constellation	la constelación
cosmic	cósmico, -a
cosmos	el cosmos
eclipse	el eclipse
flying saucer	el platillo volador
galaxy	la galaxia
globe (of the Earth)	el globo de la Tierra
to gravitate	gravitar
meteor	el meteoro
the Milky Way	la Vía Láctea
moon	la luna
orbit	la órbita
oxygen	el oxígeno
planet	el planeta
rotation	la rotación
satellite	el satélite
sky	el cielo
solar system	el sistema solar
spaceship	la nave espacial
space station	la estación espacial
spatial	espacial
star	la estrella
sun	el sol
UFO	el OVNI
universal	universal
universe	el universo
weightlessness	la ingravidez

Planet Earth	**El planeta tierra**
Land	*La tierra*
altitude	la altitud
atlas	el atlas
cave	la cueva

Land (cont.)	La tierra (cont.)
cliff	el acantilado
coast	la costa
continent	el continente
crater	el cráter
desert	el desierto
dune	la duna
forest	el bosque
hill	la colina
jungle	la selva
landscape	el paisaje
mountain	la montaña
nature	la naturaleza
peninsula	la península
plain	el llano
plateau	la meseta
rock	la roca
rocky	rocoso, -a
sand	la arena
shore	la orilla
surface	la superficie
terrestrial	terrestre
valley	el valle
volcano	el volcán

Water	El agua
beach	la playa
brook	el arroyo
canal	el canal
cascade	la cascada
current	la corriente
glacier	el glaciar
navigable	navegable
pond	el estanque
river	el río
spring	el manantial
tide	la marea
torrent	el torrente
wave	la ola

Weather and the seasons	El clima y las estaciones
breeze	la brisa
clear	despejado, -a
cloud	la nube
cloudy	nublado, -a
cold	el frío
cool	el fresco
downpour	el aguacero
drizzle	la llovizna
fall	el otoño
fog	la niebla
to freeze	helar
frost	la escarcha
heat	el calor

Weather and the seasons (cont.)

lightning bolt	el rayo
rainbow	el arco iris
shower	el aguacero
snow (noun)	la nieve
to snow	nevar
spring	la primavera
summer	el verano
sunny	soleado, -a
thaw (noun)	el deshielo
to thaw	descongelar
thunder (noun)	el trueno
to thunder	tronar
wind	el viento
windy	ventoso
winter	el invierno

El clima y las estaciones (cont.)

Disasters and severe conditions

avalanche	la avalancha
drought	la sequía
flood	la inundación
hurricane	el huracán
lava	la lava
storm	la tormenta
tornado	el tornado
tsunami	el tsunami

Los desastres y las condiciones severas

Weather report

average	medio, -a
change	el cambio
continental	continental
degree	el grado
disturbance	la perturbación
to drop	bajar
forecast	el pronóstico
minus	menos
plus	plus
rain (noun)	la lluvia
to rain	llover
report	el reporte
rise (noun)	la subida
to rise	subir
shade	la sombra
to shine	brillar
sunrise	el amanecer
sunset	el atardecer
temperature	la temperatura
variable	variable
zone	la zona

El informe del tiempo

Farming, gardening, and tools

agriculturist	el agricultor, la agricultora
to breed	criar
breeder	el criador, la criadora

La agricultura, la jardinería y los utensilios

Farming, gardening, and tools (cont.)

La agricultura, la jardinería y los utensilios (cont.)

cattle	el ganado
country	el campo
to cultivate	cultivar
fertile	fértil
to fertilize	abonar
fertilizer	el abono
fruit	la fruta
to fumigate	fumigar
garden	el jardín
to graze	pacer
to grow	crecer
harvest (noun)	la cosecha
to harvest	cosechar
hose	la manguera
insecticide	el insecticida
to irrigate	irrigar
lawn	el césped
lawn mower	el cortacésped
orchard	el huerto
plow	el arado
rake (noun)	el rastrillo
to rake	rastrillar
seed	la semilla
shovel	la pala
soil	la tierra
to sow	sembrar
sprinkler	el irrigador
tractor	el tractor
vegetable	el vegetal
watering hose	la manguera

Trees

Los árboles

apple tree	el manzano
avocado tree	el aguacate
banana tree	el banano
cedar	el cedro
fig tree	la higuera
fruit tree	el árbol frutal
graft (noun)	el injerto
to graft	injertar
olive tree	el olivo
orange tree	el naranjo
palm tree	la palma

Flowers

Las flores

carnation	el clavel
daffodil	el narciso
daisy	la margarita
gardenia	la gardenia
orchid	la orquídea
plant (noun)	la planta
to plant	plantar

Flowers (cont.)	*Las flores* (cont.)
poppy	la amapola
rose	la rosa
sunflower	el girasol
tulip	el tulipán
violet	la violeta

Domestic farm animals	*Los animales domésticos en las granjas*
bull	el toro
calf	la ternera
cat	el gato, la gata
cow	la vaca
dog	el perro, la perra
duck	el pato, la pata
ewe (sheep)	la oveja
hamster	el hámster
horse	el caballo
iguana	la iguana
mouse	el ratón, la ratona
mule	la mula
parrot	la cotorra
pet	la mascota
pig	el cerdo
pony	el poni
rabbit	el conejo, la coneja
rooster	el gallo
swan	el cisne
turkey	el pavo
turtle	la tortuga

Insects	**Los insectos**
ant	la hormiga
bee	la abeja
butterfly	la mariposa
buzz (noun)	el zumbido
to buzz	zumbar
caterpillar	la oruga
centipede	el ciempiés
cricket	el grillo
flea	la pulga
fly	la mosca

Wild animals	**Los animales salvajes**
boa	la boa
cardinal	el cardinal
chimpanzee	el chimpancé
crocodile	el cocodrilo
dolphin	el delfín
elephant	el elefante, la elefanta
frog	la rana
giraffe	la jirafa
gorilla	el gorila
hippopotamus	el hipopótamo
koala	el koala

Wild animals (cont.)

lion	el león, la leona
mollusk	el molusco
monkey	el mono
nest	el nido
octopus	el pulpo
penguin	el pingüino
quetzal	el quetzal
rhinoceros	el rinoceronte
sea urchin	el erizo
shark	el tiburón
snake	la serpiente
tiger	el tigre
whale	la ballena
wolf	el lobo, la loba
zebra	la cebra

Ecology and pollution

biodegradable	biodegradable
cleanup	la limpieza
concern	la preocupación
contamination	la contaminación
coral reef	el arrecife de coral
damage (noun)	el daño
to damage	dañar
deforestation	la deforestación
degradation	la degradación
destruction	la destrucción
to disappear	desaparecer
diversity	la diversidad
drinking water	el agua potable
ecologist	el/la ecologista
ecosystem	el ecosistema
environmentalist	el defensor, la defensora del ambiente
to erode	erosionar
erosion	la erosión
extinction	la extinción
fauna	la fauna
flora	la flora
global	global
greenhouse effect	el efecto invernadero
harmful	peligroso, -a
hole	el hueco
imbalance	el desequilibrio
industrialization	la industrialización
irreversible	irreversible
to melt	derretir, derretirse
nuclear	nuclear
oil	el petróleo
oil slick	el derramamiento de petróleo
pesticide	el pesticida
pollutant	el contaminante

Los animales salvajes (cont.)

La ecología y la polución

Ecology and pollution (cont.)

to pollute — contaminar
pollution control — el control de la polución
to preserve — preservar
to protect — proteger
to recycle — reciclar
recycling — el reciclaje
spill (noun) — el derrame
to spill — derramar
wilderness — la naturaleza silvestre

La ecología y la polución (cont.)

contaminar
el control de la polución
preservar
proteger
reciclar
el reciclaje
el derrame
derramar
la naturaleza silvestre

JUEGO

14·1

Cognados. *Translate these words from English into Spanish; include the articles **el, la, los,** and **las** as necessary.*

1. irreversible _____

2. nuclear _____

3. tractor (*m.*) _____

4. hamster (*m.*) _____

5. global _____

6. astronaut (*m./f.*) _____

7. comet (*m.*) _____

8. atlas (*m.*) _____

9. fauna (*f.*) _____

10. flora (*f.*) _____

11. tornado (*m.*) _____

12. cosmos (*m.*) _____

13. eclipse (*m.*) _____

14. meteor (*m.*) _____

15. planet (*m.*) _____

16. hurricane (*m.*) _____

17. tsunami (*m.*) _____

18. iguana (*f.*) _____

19. continental _____

20. variable _____

21. biodegradable _____

22. habitat (*m.*) _____

23. pony (*m.*) _____

24. koala (*m.*) _____

25. ecologist (*m./f.*) _____

26. lava (*f.*) _____

27. canal (*m.*) _____

28. quetzal (*m.*) _____

29. boa (*f.*) _____

30. cardinal (*m.*) _____

Palabras aprendidas. *Translate these words from English into Spanish; include the articles **el**, **la**, **los**, and **las** as necessary.*

1. border (*f.*) _____

2. lake (*m.*) _____

3. ocean (*m.*) _____

4. country (*m.*) _____

5. region (*f.*) _____

6. island (*f.*) _____

7. bay (*f.*) _____

8. gulf (*m.*) _____

9. sea (*m.*) _____

10. allergy (*f.*) _____

11. garbage (*f.*) _____

12. reserve (*f.*) _____

13. chicken (*m.*) _____

14. cockroach (*f.*) _____

15. to fly _____

16. duck (*m./f.*) _____

17. pig (*m.*) _____

18. turkey (*m.*) _____

19. fish (*m.*) _____

20. gloves (*m.*) _____

Selección múltiple. *Choose the best completion for each statement.*

1. Al mediodía en la costa se puede ver ...
   a. el desierto.
   b. el arrecife de coral.
   c. la deforestación.
   d. la constelación.

2. La Tierra pertenece al ...
   a. sistema solar.
   b. platillo volador.
   c. OVNI.
   d. cielo.

3. Los desastres naturales son ...
   a. los caballos.
   b. las brisas.
   c. los estanques.
   d. las inundaciones.

4. Los animales son ...
   a. las tormentas.
   b. los pronósticos.
   c. los cisnes.
   d. las limpiezas.

5. Estos animales son insectos:
   a. los ratones.
   b. las moscas.
   c. las orquídeas.
   d. los huertos.

Algunos animales. *Write the Spanish word or phrase for each picture on the appropriate line. Include the article **el, la, los,** or **las** where necessary.*

1. _____

2. _____

3. _____

4. _____

5. _____

6. _____

7. _____

8. _____

9. _____

10. _____

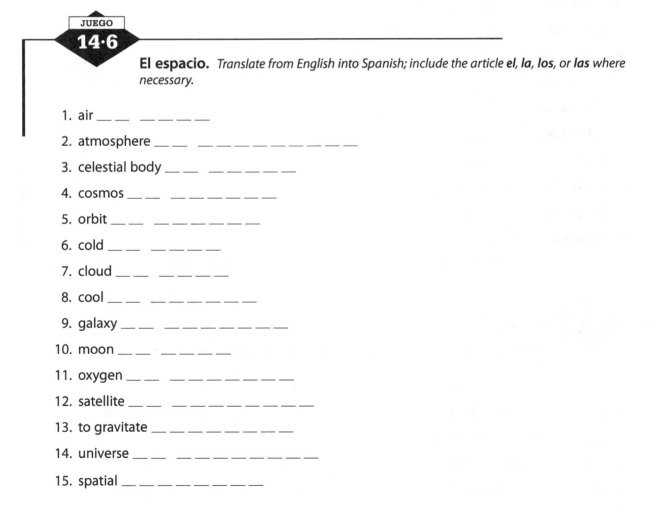

JUEGO 14·5

Un juego de palabras. *For each category below, choose the word or phrase that does not belong.*

1. **en el espacio puede encontrar** la cascada, la nave espacial, la Vía Láctea, la estación espacial

2. **los animales domésticos** la cotorra, la coneja, el perro, el rinoceronte

3. **la polución** el desequilibrio, el derramamiento de petróleo, el agua potable, el contaminante

4. **la agricultura** criar, derretir, cultivar, fumigar

5. **las flores** las gardenias, las orquídeas, las amapolas, las vacas

6. **los animales en el mar** los lobos, los delfines, los moluscos, los pulpos

7. **los árboles** el cedro, la higuera, la palma, la manguera

8. **los animales salvajes terrestres (de la tierra)** el chimpancé, el cocodrilo, el elefante, el tiburón

9. **la ecología** la protección, el efecto invernadero, el control de la polución, la naturaleza silvestre

10. **las estaciones del año** el invierno, la primavera, el otoño, la perturbación

JUEGO 14·6

El espacio. *Translate from English into Spanish; include the article el, la, los, or las where necessary.*

1. air __ __ __ __ __ __

2. atmosphere __ __ __ __ __ __ __ __ __ __ __

3. celestial body __ __ __ __ __ __ __ __

4. cosmos __ __ __ __ __ __ __ __

5. orbit __ __ __ __ __ __ __ __

6. cold __ __ __ __ __ __

7. cloud __ __ __ __ __ __

8. cool __ __ __ __ __ __ __ __

9. galaxy __ __ __ __ __ __ __ __ __

10. moon __ __ __ __ __ __

11. oxygen __ __ __ __ __ __ __ __ __

12. satellite __ __ __ __ __ __ __ __ __ __

13. to gravitate __ __ __ __ __ __ __ __

14. universe __ __ __ __ __ __ __ __ __ __

15. spatial __ __ __ __ __ __ __ __

16. weightlessness __ __ __ __ __ __ __ __ __ __ __ __

17. rotation __ __ __ __ __ __ __ __ __ __ __

18. to freeze __ __ __ __ __ __

19. windy (*m.*) __ __ __ __ __ __ __

20. avalanche __ __ __ __ __ __ __ __ __ __ __ __

Un juego acróstico. *Translate the clues on the left from English into Spanish. (You do not need to include the articles.) Reading down the first letter of each word will then reveal a Spanish word or phrase.*

1. drizzle ▨ __ __ __ __ __ __ __

2. sand ▨ __ __ __ __

3. surface ▨ __ __ __ __ __ __ __ __ __ __

4. crater ▨ __ __ __ __ __ __

5. shore ▨ __ __ __ __ __

6. navigable ▨ __ __ __ __ __ __ __ __

7. clear (*f.*) ▨ __ __ __ __ __ __ __ __

8. insecticide ▨ __ __ __ __ __ __ __ __ __ __

9. hill ▨ __ __ __ __ __

10. flood ▨ __ __ __ __ __ __ __ __ __

11. olive tree ▨ __ __ __ __

12. nature ▨ __ __ __ __ __ __ __ __ __

13. ecosystem ▨ __ __ __ __ __ __ __ __ __

14. jungle ▨ __ __ __ __

La palabra vertical: _____

Palabras. *Fill in the letters needed to complete each Spanish word or phrase.*

1. __ c __ n __ i __ a __ o (*cliff*)

2. p __ __ s __ j __ (*landscape*)

3. p __ n í __ s __ __ a (*peninsula*)

4. __ l __ i __ d (*altitude*)

5. m __ s __ __ a (*plateau*)

6. __ r r __ __ o (*brook*)

7. t __ r r __ s __ r __ (*terrestrial*)

8. r __ c __ __ a (*rocky*)

9. m __ n __ n __ i __ l (*spring*)

10. c __ r r __ e __ __ e (*current*)

11. t __ r r __ __ t __ (*torrent*)

12. __ u __ l __ __ o (*cloudy*)

13. __ __ a __ i __ __ (*glacier*)

14. __ g __ a __ __ r __ (*downpour*)

15. e __ c __ r __ __ a (*frost*)

Palabras escondidas en este juego de puzle. *Find and circle the Spanish words hidden vertically, horizontally, and diagonally.*

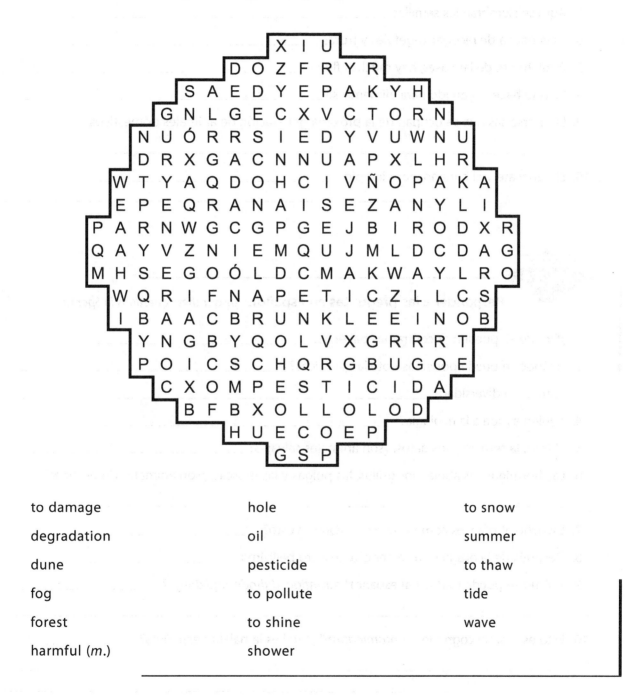

```
            X I U
          D O Z F R Y R
        S A E D Y E P A K Y H
      G N L G E C X V C T O R N
    N U Ó R R S I E D Y V U W N U
    D R X G A C N N U A P X L H R
  W T Y A Q D O H C I V Ñ O P A K A
  E P E Q R A N A I S E Z A N Y L I
P A R N W G C G P G E J B I R O D X R
Q A Y V Z N I E M Q U J M L D C D A G
M H S E G O Ó L D C M A K W A Y L R O
  W Q R I F N A P E T I C Z L L C S
  I B A A C B R U N K L E E I N O B
    Y N G B Y Q O L V X G R R R T
    P O I C S C H Q R G B U G O E
      C X O M P E S T I C I D A
        B F B X O L L O L O D
          H U E C O E P
            G S P
```

to damage	hole	to snow
degradation	oil	summer
dune	pesticide	to thaw
fog	to pollute	tide
forest	to shine	wave
harmful (*m.*)	shower	

La agricultura, la jardinería y los árboles: Adivinanza. *Guess what Spanish word or phrase corresponds to each definition or description.*

1. Para cortar el césped _____

2. Para usar el agua cuando no llueve _____

3. Un producto que ayuda a las orquídeas a florecer más _____

4. Las personas que cultivan las frutas y los vegetales _____

5. Aquí se siembran las semillas _____

6. Es la época de recoger vegetales y frutas _____

7. Aquí, frente de las casas, hay muchas flores _____

8. Lo que hace el ganado para alimentarse _____

9. Las personas que se ocupan de la próxima generación de animales dómesticos _____
_____

10. El aguacate y el banano, por ejemplo _____

Responder a las preguntas en español. *Answer these questions in Spanish.*

1. ¿Dónde se pueden encontrar las ballenas? _____

2. ¿Dónde se puede poner las botellas plásticas? _____

3. ¿Qué es la diversidad? _____

4. ¿Quién ayuda a la ecología? _____

5. El toro, la ternera y los gatos, ¿son animales salvajes? _____

6. Las hormigas, las abejas, los grillos, las pulgas y las moscas, ¿son animales domésticos? _____
_____

7. Escucho ahora y es como zzzzzzz ... ¿Qué es esto? _____

8. Después de la oruga va a crecer este insecto bellísimo. _____

9. ¿Cómo se puede traducir al espanol "*carnation, daffodil, and daisy*"? _____
_____

10. Esto es casi un cognado: "*contamination*". ¿Cuál es la palabra española? _____
_____

Palabras aprendidas. *Translate these words from English into Spanish. Reading down the boxed column will then reveal a Spanish word or phrase.*

1. cave ▪ __ __ __ __ __ __
2. rock __ __ __ __ __ ▪
3. thaw __ __ __ __ ▪ __ __ __ __
4. plow ▪ __ __ __ __ __ __
5. sunny (*m.*) ▪ __ __ __ __ __ __
6. fertile __ __ __ ▪ __ __
7. heat __ __ __ __ ▪ __ __
8. to grow __ __ __ ▪ __ __
9. to irrigate __ __ __ ▪ __ __
10. ewe __ __ ▪ __ __ __
11. frog __ __ __ __ ▪ __
12. graft __ __ __ __ ▪ __ __
13. rake __ __ __ __ ▪ __ __ __

La palabra vertical: _____

Crucigrama. *Fill in the crossword puzzle with the Spanish words.*

Horizontales (*Across*)

1. rise

4. temperature

6. drought

7. destruction

10. shade

11. greenhouse effect
(*2 words*)

14. to thunder

15. comet

18. cliff

19. spill

Verticales (*Down*)

2. weightlessness

3. sunrise

5. change

8. river

9. constellation

11. extinction

12. celestial body

13. to erode

16. to drop

17. valley

Los números, las cantidades y el tiempo

Numbers, quantities, and time

·15·

Calculation

to add
addition
to calculate
calculator
to count
difference
to divide
division
equal
for
less
minus
multiplication
to multiply
number (noun)
to number
plus
to subtract
subtraction
sum
total

El cálculo

añadir; sumar
la suma
calcular
la calculadora
contar; computar
la diferencia
dividir
la división
igual
por
menos
menos
la multiplicación
multiplicar
el número
numerar
más
restar
la resta
la suma
el total

Measures

area
breadth
capacity
centimeter
depth
dimension
foot
height
inch
kilogram
kilometer
length
liter
to measure
measurement
measuring tape

Las medidas

el área
el ancho
la capacidad
el centímetro
la profundidad
la dimensión
el pie
la altura
la pulgada
el kilogramo
el kilómetro
el largo; la longitud
el litro
medir
la medida
la cinta para medir

187

Measures (cont.)

meter	el metro
mile	la milla
millimeter	el milímetro
ruler	la regla
scale	la báscula
size	el número
surface	la superficie
tape measure	la medida en pulgadas
ton	la tonelada
volume	el volumen
to weigh	pesar
weight	el peso
width	la anchura
yard	la yarda

Numbers

Cardinal numbers

zero	cero
one	uno
two	dos
three	tres
four	cuatro
five	cinco
six	seis
seven	siete
eight	ocho
nine	nueve
ten	diez
eleven	once
twelve	doce
thirteen	trece
fourteen	catorce
fifteen	quince
sixteen	dieciséis
seventeen	diecisiete
eighteen	dieciocho
nineteen	diecinueve
twenty	veinte
twenty-one	veintiuno
twenty-two	veintidós
twenty-three	veintitrés
twenty-four	veinticuatro
twenty-five	veinticinco
twenty-six	veintiséis
twenty-seven	veintisiete
twenty-eight	veintiocho
twenty-nine	veintinueve
thirty	treinta
thirty-one	treinta y uno
thirty-two	treinta y dos
forty	cuarenta
fifty	cincuenta

Las medidas (cont.)

Los números

Los números cardinales

Cardinal numbers (cont.)	Los números cardinales (cont.)
sixty	sesenta
seventy	setenta
eighty	ochenta
ninety	noventa
one hundred	cien, ciento
one hundred and one	ciento uno, -a
two hundred	doscientos, -as
three hundred	trescientos, -as
four hundred	cuatrocientos, -as
five hundred	quinientos, -as
six hundred	seiscientos, -as
seven hundred	setecientos, -as
eight hundred	ochocientos, -as
nine hundred	novecientos, -as
one thousand	mil
two thousand	dos mil
one hundred thousand	cien mil
one million	un millón
one billion	mil millones

Ordinal numbers	Los números ordinales
first	primero, -a
second	segundo, -a
third	tercer, tercera
fourth	cuarto, -a
fifth	quinto, -a
sixth	sexto, -a
seventh	séptimo, -a
eighth	octavo, -a
ninth	noveno, -a
tenth	décimo, -a

Quantities	**Las cantidades**
bottle	la botella
box	la caja
cup	la taza
double (noun)	doble
to double	doblar
dozen	la docena
fourth	el cuarto
glass	el vaso
half (noun)	la mitad
half (adj.)	medio, -a
handful	el puñado
mouthful	el bocado
ounce	la onza
pair	el par
percent	el por ciento
percentage	el porcentaje
piece	el pedazo
pinch	la pizca
pound	la libra

Quantities (cont.)

quantity	la cantidad
slice	la rebanada
spoonful	la cucharada
teaspoon, teaspoonful	la cucharadita

Other measures and quantities; miscellaneous

Otras medidas y cantidades; palabras misceláneas

address	la dirección
a few	unos cuantos, unas cuantas
algebra	el álgebra
a little	un poco
a lot	mucho, -a
angle	el ángulo
bank card	la tarjeta del banco
birthday	el cumpleaños
birthday card	la tarjeta de cumpleaños
card game	el juego de cartas
deep	profundo, -a
double	el doble
enormous	enorme
enough	bastante; suficiente
few	pocos, -as
geometry	la geometría
gigantic	gigantesco, -a
less	menos
little	poco
mailbox	la casilla
millionaire	millonario, -a
more	más
most	la mayoría
much	mucho, -a
password	la contraseña
recipe	la receta
rhombus	el rombo
several	algunos, -as
small	pequeño, -a
so many	tantos, -as
some	algunos, -as
so much	tanto, -a
too many	demasiados, -as
wide	ancho, -a

Time

El tiempo

afternoon	la tarde
calendar	el calendario
clock	el reloj
date	la fecha
dawn	el amanecer
day	el día
day after tomorrow	pasado mañana
day before yesterday	anteayer
daybreak	la madrugada

Time (cont.)	**El tiempo (cont.)**
half hour	la media hora
hour	la hora
last night	anoche
midnight	la medianoche
month	el mes
morning	la mañana
night	la noche
noon	el mediodía
o'clock	en punto
to tell time	dar la hora
today	hoy
tomorrow	mañana
tomorrow morning	mañana por la mañana
week	la semana
weekend	el fin de semana
year	el año

Days of the week	**Los días de la semana**
Sunday	el domingo
Monday	el lunes
Tuesday	el martes
Wednesday	el miércoles
Thursday	el jueves
Friday	el viernes
Saturday	el sábado

Months of the year	**Los meses del año**
January	enero
February	febrero
March	marzo
April	abril
May	mayo
June	junio
July	julio
August	agosto
September	septiembre; setiembre
October	octubre
November	noviembre
December	diciembre

Cognados. *Translate these words from English into Spanish; include the articles **el, la, los,** and **las** as necessary.*

1. number (*m.*) _____
2. sum (*f.*) _____
3. total (*m.*) _____
4. yard (*f.*) _____
5. double (*m.*) _____
6. area (*f.*) _____
7. division (*f.*) _____
8. kilogram (*m.*) _____
9. zero _____
10. kilometer (*m.*) _____
11. double (*m.*) _____
12. capacity (*f.*) _____
13. hour (*f.*) _____
14. dimension (*f.*) _____
15. gigantic (*m.*) _____
16. to calculate _____
17. liter (*m.*) _____
18. difference (*f.*) _____
19. centimeter (*m.*) _____
20. meter (*m.*) _____

Palabras aprendidas en otros capítulos. *Translate these words from English into Spanish; include the articles* **el**, **la**, **los**, *and* **las** *as necessary.*

1. box (f.) _____

2. number (m.) _____

3. surface (f) _____

4. morning (f.) _____

5. cup (f.) _____

6. spoonful (f.) _____

7. teaspoon (f.) _____

8. much (m.) _____

9. day (m.) _____

10. address (f.) _____

11. password (f.) _____

12. recipe (f.) _____

13. Sunday (m.) _____

14. date (f.) _____

15. night (f.) _____

16. July _____

17. dawn (m.) _____

18. month (m.) _____

19. tomorrow _____

20. June _____

21. August _____

22. card game (m.) _____

23. birthday (m.) _____

24. mile (f.) _____

Selección múltiple. *Choose the best completion for each statement.*

1. El cálculo incluye ...
   a. la hora.
   b. el pasado.
   c. la resta.
   d. el mes.

2. Los números incluyen ...
   a. los cardinales.
   b. los pedazos.
   c. las libras.
   d. las rebanadas.

3. El tiempo incluye ...
   a. el milímetro.
   b. la tarde.
   c. la anchura.
   d. el largo.

4. El mes para las vacaciones es ...
   a. el jueves.
   b. la semana.
   c. la medianoche.
   d. el agosto.

5. Acerca del tiempo, es ...
   a. la tarde.
   b. la cantidad.
   c. la onza.
   d. la mitad.

Un juego de palabras. *For each phrase or category below, choose the word or phrase that **does** correspond to it.*

1. **el mediodía es** la noche, el pasado mañana, a las doce en punto, a las once y media

2. **el reloj** da la hora, da el puñado, da la pizca, da la mayoría, da algunos

3. **la suma** restar, sumar, dividir, multiplicar

4. **la medida es** contar los días, calcular números, pesar toneladas, restar los meses

5. **el pie tiene** la profundidad, las pulgadas, las alturas, la longitud

6. **contar** medir, computar, pesar, dejar

7. **los números** cardinales, botellas, novenas, meses

8. **el tiempo** la medianoche, la novena, la pulgada, la adición

9. **la cantidad** la séptima, la mitad, la madrugada, la media hora

10. **los días de la semana** doce, cinco, siete, ocho

JUEGO
15·5

Otras palabras de esta unidad. *Translate from English into Spanish; include the article **el**, **la**, **los**, or **las** as necessary.*

1. geometry __ __ __ __ __ __ __ __ __ __ __

2. algebra __ __ __ __ __ __ __ __ __

3. millionaire (*f.*) __ __ __ __ __ __ __ __ __ __ __ __

4. angle __ __ __ __ __ __ __ __

5. enough __ __ __ __ __ __ __ __

6. few (*m.*) __ __ __ __ __

7. a few (*f.*) __ __ __ __ __ __ __ __ __ __

8. a little __ __ __ __ __ __

9. a lot (of) (*m.*) __ __ __ __ __

10. more __ __ __

11. small (*m.*) __ __ __ __ __ __ __

12. so many (*f.*) __ __ __ __ __ __

13. so much (*f.*) __ __ __ __ __

14. some (*m.*) __ __ __ __ __ __ __

15. fourth __ __ __ __ __ __ __ __

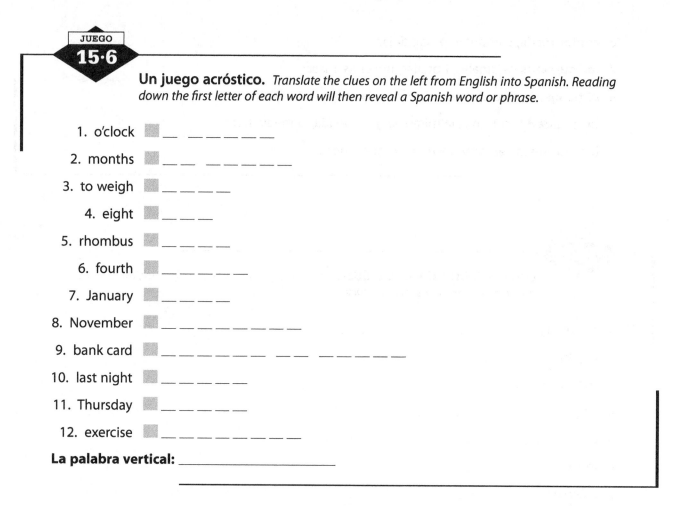

JUEGO 15·6

Un juego acróstico. *Translate the clues on the left from English into Spanish. Reading down the first letter of each word will then reveal a Spanish word or phrase.*

1. o'clock   __   __ __ __ __ __
2. months   __ __   __ __ __ __ __
3. to weigh   __ __ __ __
4. eight   __ __ __
5. rhombus   __ __ __ __
6. fourth   __ __ __ __ __
7. January   __ __ __ __
8. November   __ __ __ __ __ __ __ __
9. bank card   __ __ __ __ __ __   __ __   __ __ __ __ __ __
10. last night   __ __ __ __ __
11. Thursday   __ __ __ __ __
12. exercise   __ __ __ __ __ __ __ __

La palabra vertical: _____

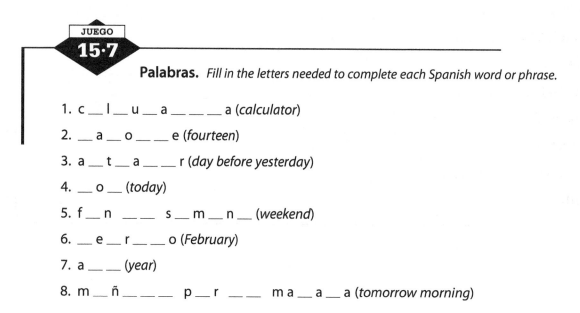

JUEGO 15·7

Palabras. *Fill in the letters needed to complete each Spanish word or phrase.*

1. c __ l __ u __ a __ __ __ a (*calculator*)
2. __ a __ o __ __ e (*fourteen*)
3. a __ t __ a __ __ r (*day before yesterday*)
4. __ o __ (*today*)
5. f __ n __ __ __ s __ m __ n __ (*weekend*)
6. __ e __ r __ __ o (*February*)
7. a __ __ (*year*)
8. m __ ñ __ __ __ __ p __ r __ __ __ m a __ a __ a (*tomorrow morning*)

9. __ o __ l __ r (*to double*)

10. t __ e __ n __ a y __ __ o (*thirty-one*)

11. b __ c __ __ o (*mouthful*)

12. __ e __ __ n __ (*week*)

13. n __ v __ e __ __ r __ (*November*)

14. __ i __ n __ __ l (*one hundred thousand*)

15. m __ r __ o (*March*)

JUEGO

15·8

Las medidas, los números y más: Adivinanza. *Guess what Spanish word or phrase corresponds to each definition or description.*

1. Para ver las libras que tenemos en cada cuerpo _____

2. Para revisar las citas que tenemos cada mes _____

3. Para enviar a una persona que tiene cumpleaños _____

4. Un aparato para sumar, dividir y más _____

5. Para medir la anchura y la altura en las paredes en los Estados Unidos _____

_____

6. Un pedazo, por ejemplo de pan _____

7. Para poner el azúcar en el café con leche _____

8. La materia que cubre ángulos y las medidas en el espacio _____

9. Para revisar las cartas y los periódicos en nuestra casa _____

10. Para sacar mi dinero en el banco _____

Palabras escondidas en este juego de puzle. *Find and circle the Spanish words hidden vertically, horizontally, and diagonally.*

```
N Y Z L T K M Q B F J W N H A W X
S X C X X P R N T L P M Y U X G M
K F R O P N M I L L O N A R I O A
W U T B N B M J G X C B Ú C W R P
G Z B D H T Z G F D T C M M O W N
W B O D S Q R B W T Q T C D E Ó C
H O T Q A S F A I B G J A O I R B
Q X E G L N P O S S D L S S R J O
B M L D P V I R M E U C I S V P X
Y M L Z I T K A O C Ñ V L B D E D
O X A U D V G I L F I A L H H D T
K E J I D E I A D D U J A G W A U
H V N X S R C D D R D N H N R Z W
O D O O E N N M I L Q S D L R O C
T O W N R E S T A R H A Z A S Q L
R V I G Z M E Z L P Z G E U O U L
Z Z R W N A E D I C I E M B R E G
```

bottle	division	ounce
calculator	enormous	password
December	mailbox	piece
deep (f.)	millionaire	to subtract
to divide	number	

Crucigrama. *Fill in the crossword puzzle with the Spanish words.*

Horizontales (*Across*)

1. handful
8. mailbox
9. mouthful
10. geometry
11. fifteen
13. capacity
15. day after tomorrow (*2 words*)
17. four

Verticales (*Down*)

2. day before yesterday
3. password
4. to weigh
5. pound
6. depth
7. daybreak
12. piece
14. to add
16. sixth (*f.*)

Answer key

1   Las comunicaciones y los medios · *Communications and media*

1·1   1. saludos   2. hasta luego / despedida   3. conocer   4. adiós   5. contestar
6. gracias   7. de nada   8. saludar   9. la dirección   10. alegre

1·2   1. actuar   2. el chip de la computadora   3. el virus   4. la identidad
5. piratear, hackear   6. eliminar   7. dramático / dramática   8. escanear
9. el bloguero / la bloguera   10. el pirata informático   11. el puzle
12. el chat   13. el clímax   14. la escena   15. el suspenso   16. la alerta
17. la tele   18. el horóscopo   19. el film   20. la comedia   21. publicar
22. el episodio   23. la prensa   24. el satélite   25. la página de la web

1·3   1. la página inicial   2. acceder   3. el ratón   4. el archivo   5. la contraseña
6. el virus   7. escanear   8. el mensaje electrónico   9. el monitor

1·4

```
M P N H I A G S K U M P E A P
S U A R A M K T V D S J J W E
M S O N L L A M A R A D I C T
A T Z W T C K L O S P Y T O G
R L B R F A Q B N I E T N C H
C O L G A R L E I V G K E T B
A M S W V G M L K A G O L R U
R N M H B A N U A C V R É A Z
F L N S B R H O R F P Q F S Ó
F B J U X N R I Z G X M O E N
P G P V B E K M Ó V I L N Ñ E
G L K C M G V I D N B C O A Z
A R N Ú P A C C E D E R C K J
T P N H L L F Z W C Ó D I G O
R E S P O N D E R D I W A C F
```

Words: acceder, responder, llamar, móvil, cargar, marcar, colgar, oigo, buzón, mensaje, número, contraseña, pantalla, teléfono, código

1·5   1. el sobre   2. el remitente   3. el sello   4. el destinatario   5. la dirección   6. el código postal   7. la carta   8. la fecha   9. el saludo   10. la despedida   11. la firma

1·6   1. a   2. b   3. c   4. c   5. a

1·7   1. cartero   2. hola   3. estampilla   4. saludo   5. nombre   6. despedida
7. colgar   8. recado   9. conocido   10. apellido   11. buzón   12. de nada

La palabra vertical: comunicación (*communication*)

1·8   1. la telenovela   2. el acomodador   3. el radioyente   4. estar feliz   5. la cucaracha   6. el dibujo animado   7. llorar   8. la pantalla   9. el chip   10. la gramática

1·9   1. cuento   2. revista   3. usuario   4. columna   5. Internet   6. gastronomía   7. reportera
8. anuncio   9. medios   10. artículo

La palabra vertical: crucigrama (*crossword*)

1·10   1. audiencia   2. telebasura   3. canales   4. registrarse a la tele   5. documental   6. estrella de cine
7. aplaudir   8. cinematografía   9. éxito   10. personaje   11. argumento   12. control remoto
13. enchufar   14. noticias de última hora

1·11   **Horizontales** (*Across*)

1. drama   8. estrella   9. final   10. audiencia   12. pantalla   17. éxito   18. emocionante
19. chistosa

Verticales (*Down*)

2. argumento   3. billete   4. doblado   5. película   6. papel   7. ensayo   10. aplauso
11. conmovedor   13. trágico   14. subtítulo   15. fracaso   16. teatro

2   De la vida humana: las relaciones, las celebraciones y las nacionalidades · *All about human life: relationships, celebrations, and nationalities*

2·1   1. impaciente   2. sentimental   3. ingenioso   4. introvertido   5. sincera   6. ridículo
7. sociable   8. indiscreto   9. inteligente   10. felices   11. arrogantes   12. paciente
13. seria   14. extrovertido

2·2

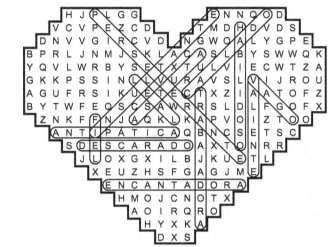

Words: encantadora, valiente, fiel, habilidoso, trabajadora, vago, leal, insultante, perseverante, callado, descarado, astuta, antipática

2·3   1. África   2. La Habana   3. Asia   4. un filipino / una filipina   5. griego   6. Dinamarca
7. Europa   8. Australia   9. Rumania   10. Roma   11. Holanda   12. Suecia   13. Canadá
14. nicaragüense   15. Buenos Aires

2·4   1. d   2. b   3. d   4. b   5. d

2·5   1. el niño menor   2. los tíos   3. la hija mayor   4. infiel   5. antipático   6. descarada
7. perseverante   8. trabajador   9. las tías   10. habilidosa   11. insultante   12. brusco
13. astuta   14. las sobrinas   15. el divorcio

2·6   1. merienda   2. desayuno   3. pastel   4. cena   5. queso   6. budín de pan   7. merengue
8. almuerzo   9. chocolate   10. café   11. champán   12. bebidas

La palabra vertical: dulce de leche

2·7   1. la ciudadanía   2. el ateo   3. crearse   4. insultante   5. los emprendedores   6. la silla
7. el descarado   8. el valiente   9. Marruecos   10. tío

2·8   1. yerno   2. pariente   3. primo   4. nuera   5. abuelas   6. prometida   7. hijastro   8. suegra
9. esposa   10. adoptar   11. padrastro   12. abuelos   13. nieto   14. familia política   15. padrino

2·9 1. libio 2. libanesa 3. europeo 4. venezolana 5. argentino 6. rumana 7. sueco
8. ecuatoriana 9. bélgico 10. irlandesa 11. estoniano 12. nicaragüense

La palabra vertical: llevarse bien (*to get along*)

2·10 *Answers may vary.* 1. ¿Cuál es la capital de Haití? 2. ¿Cuál es la capital de Colombia? 3. ¿Cuál es la capital de Paraguay? 4. ¿Cuál es la capital de Chile? 5. ¿Cuál es la capital de España? 6. ¿Cuál es la capital de Gran Bretaña? 7. ¿Cuál es la moneda de Canadá? 8. ¿Cuál es la moneda de los Estados de la Unión Europea? 9. ¿Cuál es la moneda de los Estados Unidos? 10. ¿Cuál es la moneda de Gran Bretaña?

2·11 **Horizontales** (*Across*)

4. nacimiento 7. padrino 8. casarse 9. matrimonio 11. fiesta 12. acontecimiento
15. pariente 16. misa 17. celebrar 18. piñata 19. confeti 20. suegro

Verticales (*Down*)

1. hijastra 2. velitas 3. boda 5. tradición 6. bautismo 8. comprometerse 10. relación
13. cumpleaños 14. champán 16. madrina

3 El cuerpo humano, la salud y la higiene · *The human body, health, and hygiene*

3·1 1. la cabeza 2. el cuello 3. el hombro 4. el pecho 5. el brazo 6. el codo 7. la mano
8. los dedos 9. las uñas 10. el pulgar, el dedo gordo 11. el vientre, la barriga 12. la cintura
13. el muslo 14. la rodilla 15. la pierna 16. el tobillo 17. el pie

3·2 1. la altura 2. el músculo 3. la pierna 4. pesada 5. delgado 6. morena 7. pecoso
8. la cicatriz 9. el lunar 10. calvo 11. rubia 12. el pelo lacio 13. pelirrojo 14. los dientes
15. las muelas

3·3 1. d 2. b 3. a 4. c 5. a

3·4 *Answers may vary.* 1. las tijeras 2. el hilo dental 3. hacer gárgaras 4. la peluquería / la barbería
5. el cortauñas 6. la cuchilla de afeitar / la máquina de afeitar eléctrica 7. la bañera 8. en buena
forma física 9. la buena salud mental 10. la medicina preventiva 11. el desodorante
12. el pañuelo de papel

3·5 1. el corazón 2. la vejiga 3. la estatura 4. el ombligo 5. los huesos 6. la muñeca
7. el vello 8. la pierna 9. el pulgar / el dedo gordo 10. el hombro 11. el índice
12. el puño 13. el codo 14. el esqueleto 15. la piel

3·6 1. la basura 2. sano 3. el talón 4. el pecho 5. regordete 6. la pantorrilla
7. la amígdala 8. la mandíbula 9. el dedo 10. la pantorrilla

3·7 1. cepillarse 2. el hilo dental 3. el enjuague bucal 4. jabonarse 5. la menstruación
6. el mondadientes 7. el corte de pelo 8. la lima de uñas 9. el peine 10. la caspa
11. la toalla 12. lavar 13. el olor del cuerpo 14. la espuma 15. malsano

3·8 1. la nariz 2. la nuca 3. la patilla 4. el cuello 5. la pestaña 6. la cicatriz 7. la piel
8. la ceja 9. el paladar 10. la encía 11. la lengua 12. el colmillo 13. la mejilla 14. la oreja

La palabra vertical: la pupila del ojo (*pupil*)

3·9 1. lavar 2. aseo 3. hígado 4. intestino 5. gárgara 6. incisivo 7. encía
8. nudillo 9. empeine 10. barba 11. uñas 12. crema 13. ampolla 14. lunar

La palabra vertical: la higiene bucal (*oral hygiene*)

3·10 *Answers may vary.* 1. ¿Qué hacemos para oír? 2. ¿Qué hacemos con la vista?
3. ¿Qué podemos constatar a través del olfato? 4. ¿Qué podemos verificar a través del tacto?
5. ¿Qué es una comida saludable / sana? 6. ¿Qué es una persona vigorosa? 7. ¿Qué es una chica
enfermiza / malsana? 8. ¿Qué es la ampolla? / ¿Qué es el callo? 9. ¿Qué son los piojos?
10. ¿Qué es el cortaúñas? 11. ¿Qué es el champú? 12. ¿Qué es la crema / la loción para la piel?

3·11 1. cerebro 2. párpado 3. frente 4. peca 5. canosa 6. trasero 7. corazón 8. saludable
9. prevenir 10. ejercicio 11. desodorante 12. esponja 13. loción 14. tijeras 15. piojos

3·12

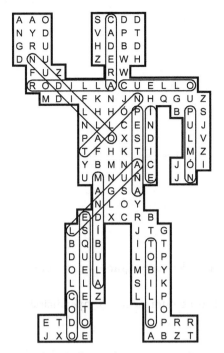

Words: tobillo, codo, pestaña, talón, cadera, índice, mandíbula, rodilla, nudillo, pulmón, cuello, esqueleto, lengua

3·13 **Horizontales** (*Across*)

1. vigorosa   7. champú   10. mondadientes   12. afeitarse   13. esqueleto   15. cicatriz
16. saludable   18. arruga   20. gárgara   21. tijeras   22. cintura

Verticales (*Down*)

2. sentido   3. bañarse   4. caspa   5. loción   6. delgada   8. peluquería   9. bienestar
10. musculosa   11. toalla   14. espuma   17. bigote   19. gordo

4   Las enfermedades y el cuidado médico · *Illnesses and medical care;* Las etapas de la vida · *Stages of life*

4·1   1. la diabetes   2. la artritis   3. el asma   4. la demencia   5. la vitamina   6. la inyección
7. la bronquitis   8. el alcoholismo   9. el doctor, la doctora   10. la mariguana
11. la anorexia   12. la bulimia   13. el reuma / el reumatismo   14. la cocaína / la coca
15. la neurosis   16. el hospital   17. el laxante   18. la operación   19. la adicción
20. el estrés

4·2   1. el cerebro   2. el hueso   3. la oreja   4. la urgencia   5. el dolor de muela   6. la muela
7. el consultorio   8. el brazo   9. el corazón   10. la pierna   11. la farmacia
12. las amígdalas   13. las gafas / los lentes / los espejuelos   14. la lengua   15. el cuerpo
16. el intestino

4·3   1. g   2. d   3. h   4. a   5. j   6. e   7. l   8. i   9. n   10. c   11. m   12. b
13. k   14. f

4·4   1. g   2. i   3. j   4. b   5. a   6. h   7. d   8. c   9. f   10. e

4·5   1. d   2. a   3. d   4. c   5. a

4·6   1. el velorio   2. el pésame   3. el luto   4. la vida   5. el testamento   6. la jubilación   7. el epitafio
8. la muerte   9. el entierro   10. fallecer   11. el cementerio   12. la heredera   13. vivir
14. la agonía   15. la cremación

4·7   1. V   2. V   3. F   4. F   5. V   6. F   7. F   8. V   9. F   10. V   11. F   12. F

4·8

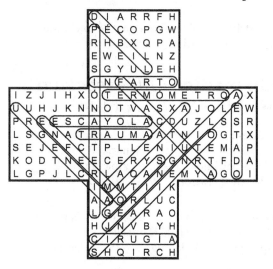

```
X E I P Z B D S O V L O O A K
M A R E O E O C R H Z N Z R B
W Q A I J T L Q L N A R A C N
E H L A D U O E X R E R A A Q
M T Q V L S R T G C O L N L D
P R S P Z N M M N J Y S R L O
E S S A S X U Á E Z H H T O L
O B J K N D C M H X U A I C E
R O P B Q G V P M E A E F D R
A Y K R V Y R F I E B R E C P
R M W N E W F A B Y L B I E J
I A H K Q K O Q R O S Q D F R
S N S U F R I R H Q X H C A G
Q T K K S N Y D V Ó M I T O B
H A T E L R F P W G M T R O E
```

Words: manta, sangrar, cáncer, callo, tos, mareo, fiebre, mejorar, doler, dolor, grano, sufrir, vómito, empeorar

4·9   1. lentillas   2. adultez   3. cumpleaños   4. asma   5. trastorno estomacal   6. apendicitis
7. reanimar   8. antibiótico   9. terapeuta   10. anorexia

La palabra vertical: la catarata (*cataract*)

4·10   **Horizontales** (*Across*)

1. funeral   3. pomada   7. enterrar   8. flemón   10. cenizas   11. infección   14. migraña
15. morir   16. parir

Verticales (*Down*)

2. retiro   4. dolencia   5. herencia   6. placa   9. etapa   12. flúor   13. niñez   14. medicina

4·11

```
        D I A R R F H
        P E C O P G W
        R H B X Q P A
        E W E I L N Z
        S G Y U L E H
        I N F A R T O
I Z J I H X Ó T E R M Ó M E T R O A X
U H J K N N O T V A S X A J O L E W
P R E E S C A Y O L A C D U Z L S R
L S G N A T R A U M A A T N I O T X
S E J E F C T P L L E N I U T E M A
K O D T N E C E R Y S G N R T F D O
L G P J L C R L A O A N E M Y A G I
        I M M T I U C
        A A O R L U C
        L G E A R A O
        H J N V B Y H
        C I R U G Í A
        S H Q I R C H
```

Words: presión arterial, sin aliento, escayola, estado, mareada, gotas, urgencia, fractura, infarto, enfermo, cirugía, jeringuilla, termómetro, trauma, débil

5   La casa y el domicilio · *House and home*

5·1   1. la televisión digital   2. el refrigerador   3. la terraza   4. eléctrico / eléctrica   5. el apartamento
6. el parque   7. el patio   8. el/la agente   9. la cortina   10. el clóset   11. reparar   12. la barbacoa
13. el aire acondicionado   14. el condominio   15. el sofá   16. el bidé   17. la agencia   18. el depósito
19. el horno   20. el congelador

5·2   1. manzana   2. pasillo   3. seguridad   4. calle   5. urbanización   6. barrio   7. vivienda
8. apartamento   9. edificio   10. hogar

5·3   1. b   2. c   3. d   4. a   5. c

5·4   1. barrer   2. negar   3. la almohada   4. la hipoteca   5. el papel higiénico   6. lavar las ropas   7. el domicilio   8. la furgoneta   9. la llave de agua   10. la lámpara

5·5   1. sótano   2. alquiler   3. toldo   4. plancha   5. chimenea   6. techo   7. triturador   8. salida   9. fregadero   10. vivienda   11. librero   12. garaje   13. cerradura   14. calefacción   15. microondas

5·6   1. el baño   2. el colchón   3. el cuarto para guardar y lavar la ropa   4. la entrada   5. el comedor   6. la cocina   7. la sala   8. la mesita de noche   9. el dormitorio, el cuarto para dormir   10. el baño   11. la terraza   12. el pasillo   13. la tetera   14. la cucharita

5·7   1. quitar la mesa   2. arreglar   3. ordenar   4. lavar la ropa   5. sacudir el polvo   6. planchar   7. hacer la cama   8. fregar el piso   9. pasar la aspiradora   10. sacar la basura   11. escurrir los platos   12. barrer

5·8   *Answers may vary.*   1. ¿Qué vista vemos por la ventana?   2. ¿Por qué tenemos un pasillo?   3. ¿Qué es un sótano?   4. ¿Qué es un garaje?   5. ¿Qué es una inmobiliaria?   6. ¿Quién es un dueño / una dueña?   7. ¿Qué es una hipoteca? / ¿Qué es un préstamo?   8. ¿Qué es *vender*?   9. ¿Qué es una brocha?   10. ¿Qué es un serrucho?   11. ¿Qué es un martillo?   12. ¿Qué es un destornillador?

5·9   1. encimera   2. lavaplatos   3. toalla de papel   4. refrigerador   5. instalar   6. toalla   7. urbanización   8. reparar   9. aparador   10. delantal   11. olla   12. recipiente   13. documento de propiedad   14. espejo   15. basura   16. abrebotellas   17. sartén   18. usos   19. ropa   20. aspiradora

La respuesta vertical: el triturador de basura (*garbage disposal*)

5·10

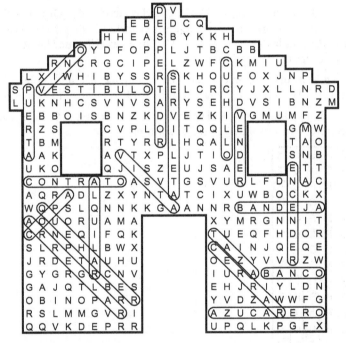

Words: despertador, banco, manta, taza, puerta, vestíbulo, quehacer, cuchillo, contrato, cerrar, servilleta, alquilar, vender, azucarero, arreglar, bandeja, encender, vista, vino, copa

5·11   **Horizontales** (*Across*)

5. toalla   8. secadora de pelo   10. taburete   12. jabonera   13. botiquín   14. perchero

Verticales (*Down*)

1. cesto de ropa   2. taza   3. clóset   4. escoba   6. llave de agua   7. florero   9. ambientador   11. cajón

5·12   1. the fifth floor (= the fourth floor American style)   2. at home   3. the balcony   4. to go up and down   5. the towel on the towel rack   6. a glass of wine   7. the first floor, the ground floor   8. house for sale   9. the hot water faucet   10. the dining room table   11. apartment for rent   12. a gas stove / a gas range   13. to turn on the washing machine   14. breakfast   15. move (***noun***) / moving

6   La comida · *Food;* En el supermercado · *At the supermarket*

6·1   1. la lechuga (*lettuce*)   2. la calabaza (*pumpkin*)   3. la cebolla (*onion*)   4. la alcachofa (*artichoke*)   5. el apio (*celery*)   6. el pepino (*cucumber*)   7. los guisantes (*peas*)   8. el maíz (*corn*)

6·2   1. persuadir   2. la promoción   3. la publicidad   4. la mayonesa   5. la mostaza   6. la papa / la patata   7. el salmón   8. la sardina   9. el atún   10. la banana   11. orgánico / orgánica   12. la mermelada   13. el cereal   14. el limón   15. la mandarina   16. el mango   17. el melón   18. el tomate   19. el café   20. el té   21. el chocolate   22. el jamón   23. el filete   24. la oliva

6·3   1. el anuncio   2. atractivo   3. gratis   4. el volante   5. anunciar   6. la marca   7. la campaña   8. la apertura   9. el catálogo   10. cerrar   11. barata   12. costoso   13. las tiendas   14. gastar   15. atraer

6·4   1. d   2. b   3. d   4. b   5. a

6·5   1. la farmacia   2. el diseño de moda   3. el lenguado   4. la leche   5. el apio   6. las cebollas   7. el salmón   8. la avena   9. la trucha   10. vender

6·6   1. langosta   2. orégano   3. sandía   4. harina   5. espinaca   6. lechuga   7. arroz   8. durazno   9. ostra   10. sabor

       La respuesta vertical: los helados (*ice cream*)

6·7   1. pelar   2. saltear   3. parrilla   4. cocinar al vapor   5. fresa   6. calabacín   7. calabaza   8. vegetal   9. pera   10. piña   11. guisante   12. hoja de laurel   13. mantequilla   14. hornear   15. naranjas

6·8   1. ¿Qué es el cupón de descuento?   2. ¿Qué es el dinero?   3. ¿Qué es el recibo?   4. ¿Quién es el/la cliente?   5. ¿Qué es el guacamole?   6. ¿Qué es sazonar?   7. ¿Qué es el aceite?   8. ¿Qué es la leche?   9. ¿Qué es el carrito de compras?   10. ¿Qué es la degustación?   11. ¿Quién es el/la guardia de seguridad?   12. ¿Qué es el mercado de pulgas?

6·9   1. coliflor   2. zanahoria   3. higo   4. toronja   5. manzana   6. berenjena   7. alcachofa   8. miel   9. remolacha   10. brócoli   11. pepino   12. ajos   13. mantequilla   14. azúcar   15. vinagre

6·10   1. el buzón de quejas   2. las gangas   3. la panadería   4. la carnicería   5. la caja   6. la pescadería   7. el delicatessen   8. la salida de incendio   9. el volante   10. la confitería

6·11

```
C T M R K B E C D Q V Q B P U F X
X Q Y L H S S X Z G M T S C I V T
Q K B Z Q D P U U F I P I K F D A
X Z E E S Q E K U U B I O Y Q S D
E I Y P K R C A C X A I I B E Q N
J U N X B X I F C D I J G R L Q N
B J C C M S A X O E P H F U Q X A
T C U O C Y S P E L I A F N Q G Y
L H T U C Y E N F O C T N F U F D
A G F K V I A O H J S E H S R T
Y E S E F N N Y U C R C F A I F
P H I A P A K A Q E J E L R L J F
T U H O L I U Y R V L W Q H T O V
A Q K L N D Ñ X W O U H D E E L X
Z K E W H H G A Z S C U C H A R A
A V C A L A B A C I N H M X R N D
A Q G C I R U E L A F P K X Q S X
```

       Words: frijol, cocinar, taza, huevos, avellana, lechuga, aceite, piña, ciruela, saltear, especias, cuchara, fresa, calabacín

6·12   1. lista de compras   2. cerveza   3. fruta   4. lomo de cerdo   5. chorizo   6. arroz   7. vino   8. salmón   9. atún   10. espárrago   11. camarón   12. maní   13. calamar

       La palabra vertical: la floristería (*flower shop*)

6·13   **Horizontales** (*Across*)

       1. cambio   6. ganga   8. cerrada   10. precio   12. gratis   13. venta   15. anunciar   17. billete   18. salida

1. cliente   2. mercancía   3. plástico   4. pago   5. apertura   7. medir   9. degustación
11. confitería   12. gastar   13. vender   14. abrir   16. costar

7   Las compras y las tiendas · *Shopping and stores;* Las ropas y otros productos personales · *Clothes and other personal items*

7·1
1. el costo   2. el crédito   3. el elevador   4. la colonia   5. el perfume   6. la crema/la loción
7. angular   8. beige   9. el permanente   10. la esmeralda   11. el gel   12. el triángulo
13. triangular   14. el violeta   15. el spray   16. el champú   17. el panty   18. el short
19. el uniforme   20. la manicura   21. la perla   22. el rubí   23. la sandalia   24. los jeans
25. rectangular   26. confortable   27. elegante   28. circular   29. el color   30. casual

7·2

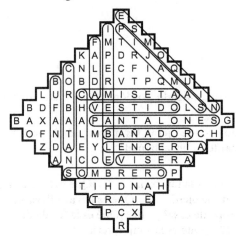

Words: vestido, sombrero, lencería, pijamas, pantalones, impermeable, bufanda, falda, traje, visera, bañador, camiseta, corbata, esmoquin, chaleco

7·3
1. d   2. b   3. a   4. b   5. c

7·4
1. teñir   2. el rímel   3. los gemelos   4. la gorra   5. el collar   6. la sudadera   7. la blusa
8. las zapatillas   9. las medias   10. las botas   11. el cinturón   12. las mallas   13. el monedero
14. la chaqueta   15. la bata de casa

7·5
1. estampado   2. chillona   3. algodón   4. guantes   5. pañuelo   6. pajarita   7. falda
8. esmeralda   9. rectángulo   10. negro   11. círculo   12. rosado   13. blanco   14. lino
15. arreglo

La palabra vertical: el agua de colonia (*eau de cologne*)

7·6
1. ropa de etiqueta   2. ir a la boda   3. los zapatos   4. las viseras   5. el escaparate
6. la mesa de noche   7. la alpargata   8. el pintalabios   9. la talla   10. el botón

7·7
1. bisutería   2. zapatería   3. librería   4. envolver   5. a plazos   6. ferretería   7. empeñar
8. dorado   9. abrigo   10. moda   11. probador   12. perchero   13. redondo   14. cuadrado
15. de moda

7·8
1. estante   2. escaparate   3. bolsas   4. prenda de vestir   5. sortija   6. joyas   7. gafas
8. anillo   9. agujero   10. botón   11. colonia   12. colorete   13. antiarrugas   14. acetona
15. pinzas

7·9
1. librería   2. oro   3. sastrería   4. envolver   5. sandalia   6. tapicería   7. anillo   8. brazalete
9. lavar   10. elevador   11. crédito   12. irregular   13. mueblería   14. impermeable   15. estrecha
16. novia   17. terciopelo   18. ojos   19. seda

La palabra vertical: los establecimientos (*establishments*)

7.10

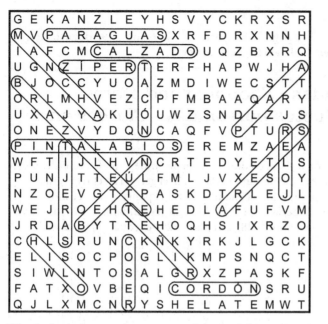

```
G E K A N Z L E Y H S V Y C K R X S R
M V P A R A G U A S X R F D R X N N H
I A F C M C A L Z A D O U Q Z B X R Q
U G N Z I P E R T E R F H A P W J H A
B J O C C Y U O A Z M D I W E C S T T
O R L M H V E Z C P F M B A A Q A R Y
U X A J A K U Ó U W Z S N D L Z J S
O N E Z V Y D Q N C A Q F V P T U R S
P I N T A L A B I O S E R E M Z A E A
W F T I J L H V N C R T E D Y E T L S
P U N J T T E Ú L F M L J V X E S O Y
N Z O E V G T T P A S K D T R L E J L
W E J R O E H T E H E D L A F U F V M
J R D A B Y T T E H O Q H S I X R Z O
C H L S R U N C K Ñ K Y R K J L G C K
E L I S O C P O G L I K M P S N Q C T
S I W L N T O S A L G R X Z P A S K F
F A T X O V B E Q I C O R D Ó N S R U
Q J L X M C N R Y S H E L A T E M W T
```

Words: brazalete, teñir, aretes, tacón, pintalabios, tijeras, coser, calzado, cordón, betún, plata, mancha, hilo, paraguas, reloj, zíper

7.11   1. el bolsillo   2. el esmalte de uñas   3. la aguja y el hilo   4. la tijera / las tijeras   5. la perfumería
6. el impermeable / el paraguas   7. el betún   8. los guantes   9. el bañador
10. el rojo, el blanco y el azul

7.12   1. ¿Qué es la heladería?   2. ¿Qué es la ferretería?   3. ¿Qué es la tapicería?   4. ¿Qué es la tienda de novias?   5. ¿Qué es probar / probarse?   6. ¿Qué es quedarle bien?   7. ¿Qué es llevar / llevarse?
8. ¿Qué es devolver?   9. ¿Qué es el departamento de la ropa de casa?   10. ¿Qué es la funda de almohada?   11. ¿Qué es el departamento de señoras?   12. ¿Qué es la sombrerería?

7.13   **Horizontales** (*Across*)

4. calzado   5. pinzas   7. manicura   8. morado   9. perchero   10. arreglo   11. envolver
12. bisutería   15. probador   16. lencería   17. grandes almacenes   18. agujero

Verticales (*Down*)

1. vender   2. talla   3. desgarrón   6. rosada   7. medir   8. mueblería   11. escaparate   13. tacón
14. botón

8   El transporte y la ciudad · *Transportation and the city*

8.1   1. el accidente   2. la bici / la bicicleta   3. el bus / el autobús   4. el seguro   5. el convertible   6. raro
7. la avenida   8. el robot   9. el banco   10. el restaurante   11. el hospital   12. la clínica
13. la mezquita   14. la estación de policía   15. la sinagoga   16. el templo   17. el tren   18. el vehículo
19. el tráfico   20. el túnel   21. acelerar   22. la alarma   23. el motor   24. el pedal
25. el radiador   26. la batería   27. reparar   28. la gasolina   29. la mecánica   30. parquear / estacionar

8.2   1. el tren   2. el carro / el auto   3. el metro / el subterráneo   4. la moto   5. la bici / la bicicleta
6. el bus / el autobús   7. el taxi   8. el escúter

8.3   1. d   2. b   3. a   4. a   5. c

8.4   1. la llanta   2. el parabrisas   3. el maletero   4. la ventanilla   5. el techo   6. el asiento   7. el timón
8. el espejo   9. las luces   10. el guantero / la guantera   11. la bocina   12. el capó   13. la ignición
14. la marcha   15. el parachoques

8.5   1. el manual del auto   2. el embrague   3. el túnel   4. el consultorio   5. el mareo   6. el volante
7. la gasolina   8. la cuesta   9. el peatón   10. encender el poste de luz

8.6   1. luces intermitentes   2. abrochar   3. choque   4. ayudar   5. luces   6. llantas   7. espejo
8. control automático   9. embotellamiento   10. rotonda   11. recoger   12. autopista   13. doblar
14. asientos

La palabra vertical: la calle cerrada (*dead-end street*)

8·7 1. carro híbrido 2. iglesia 3. alrededores 4. cerca 5. caminar 6. recoger 7. acelerar 8. parar 9. túnel 10. freno 11. millaje 12. pasajera 13. arrancar 14. maletero 15. grúa

8·8 1. camión 2. cercanía 3. subterráneo 4. furgoneta 5. picop 6. autocar 7. cruce 8. carril 9. carretera 10. atropellar 11. conductor 12. timón 13. parabrisas 14. matrícula 15. parachoques

8·9 1. estacionar 2. acelerar 3. vehículo 4. espejo 5. cascos 6. camiones 7. guantero 8. distribuidor 9. alarma 10. poner la gasolina 11. mecánico / mecánica 12. filtro para gasolina

La respuesta vertical: el vecindario (*neighborhood*)

8·10

```
M X G P C N E U M Á T I C O O Q U Z I K X
X I A C F Q H F Z A X J A V C T I O P I F
M T S W T Y T F X J Q F I B R T M P E L H
I P O R E V Z F J T P S T O B Q T J A Q X
K E L Y E K J L L B Y D J V Y J V F T S O
W L I F J S G G B A M M P U A G A K Ó Q I
V R N P O P I W N O N L K Z Q T H X N K R
E M E M V O D D F E O D F G L V T L N O M
C N R K W J O F E N H D A U B A M T R V N
I F A D N T B J A N N A M P F E F T N Z V
N Q S A B Y L I B O C A Y I I D L E L D E
O O A L R X A V I L N I V F R I O V J B L
W A Q U O S R C É I X U A J F U O G V T O
U X Y S C D A É U N C S O Y H X D E T G C
F S B E E I T Q P N T H R J S B Q C Z G I
R W T P V V S Q M A V A A A T A S C O B D
J T S S Y E U X U V R N N Q R V Q F F P A
O É E Y Y L G K A F V A L I U Z I U N E D
C O X N U W I G I Y W N R A L E I M S A C
A V H I A X S Z B H N A Q J G L C Y K J D
T N I Y X J H E S X H J O A H O A D D E U
```

Words: esquina, choque, desviación, filtro, multa, gasolinera, lago, césped, vecino, peatón, reparar, residencia, velocidad, neumático, peaje, atasco, doblar, ventanilla

8·11 1. el casco 2. el alumbrado público 3. el freno / el pedal de freno 4. el coche de bebé 5. la puerta 6. en el auto 7. el espejo retrovisor 8. el semáforo 9. el maletero 10. el consultorio

8·12 1. ¿Qué es el chofer? 2. ¿Qué es la oficina del dentista? 3. ¿Qué es el barrio protegido? 4. ¿Qué es la escuela? 5. ¿Qué es la bocina? 6. ¿Qué es el mapa? / ¿Qué es el mapa electrónico? 7. ¿Qué es un peatón? / ¿Qué es una peatona? 8. ¿Qué es la licencia de manejar? 9. ¿Qué es la gasolinera? 10. ¿Qué es el distribuidor de autos? 11. ¿Qué es el mantenimiento del auto? 12. ¿Qué es el cable para cargar la batería?

8·13 **Horizontales** (*Across*)

2. puente 3. ayudar 4. tren 5. aviso 7. lejos 8. válvula 10. mareo 11. derecha 12. parabrisas 15. radiador 16. bocina 17. reparación

Verticales (*Down*)

1. ventanilla 2. pedal 5. acelerar 6. calle 9. cuesta 10. mapa 11. desviación 13. motor 14. apurar

9 Los viajes y el turismo · *Travel and tourism*

9·1 1. abrocharse los cinturones 2. la salida de emergencia 3. abrocharse 4. el túnel 5. la salida 6. la milla 7. la silla de ruedas 8. el cheque de viajero 9. la agencia de viajes 10. la agente 11. el mar 12. el motel 13. el asiento 14. el cinturón de seguridad 15. la velocidad 16. la ventanilla 17. el aparcamiento / el estacionamiento 18. el pasajero 19. la promoción 20. la manta / la frazada 21. el precio 22. alquilar 23. la moneda 24. el control

9·2   1. el turista   2. la inmigración   3. la inmunización   4. el pasaporte   5. la visa   6. el jet   7. la seguridad   8. la terminal   9. el plan   10. el helicóptero   11. exótico   12. el tour   13. el aeropuerto   14. la recepción   15. planear   16. la cabina   17. la piloto   18. la turbulencia   19. el tren   20. el yate   21. confortable   22. la recepción   23. la suite   24. declarar   25. el capitán   26. flotar   27. el puerto   28. el hotel   29. el servicio   30. internacional

9·3   1. c   2. a   3. a   4. a   5. d

9·4   1. la cama   2. la llegada   3. el mareo   4. el baño   5. el barco   6. la caravana   7. el botones   8. el trasatlántico   9. el aeropuerto   10. la marea

9·5   1. aduana   2. frontera   3. llegada   4. facturado   5. disponible   6. quejarse   7. despegar   8. preparar   9. programar   10. pasillo   11. mareo   12. altura   13. velocidad   14. litera   15. andén

9·6   1. el embarque   2. el cargo   3. el retraso   4. desembarcar   5. el vuelo lleno   6. el viaje organizado   7. la puerta de embarque   8. disfrutar   9. millas aéreas   10. el vuelo nacional   11. la excursión   12. el destino   13. la tarjeta de crédito   14. el viaje   15. la visita guiada   16. el impuesto   17. el asiento disponible   18. el aterrizaje   19. la carga   20. el vuelo directo   21. a la hora prevista   22. el billete de ida y vuelta   23. la recompensa   24. el mostrador   25. la pista   26. la presión del aire

9·7

Words: agente, disponibilidad, folleto, tranvía, queja, copiloto, comedor, salida, guía, locomotora, equipaje, pasajero, horario, temporada, vacaciones

9·8   *Answers may vary.*   1. la maleta   2. el control de seguridad   3. la bolsa para el mareo   4. el pasillo   5. los auriculares   6. el compartimiento superior   7. la parte trasera   8. el viaje transoceánico   9. el servicio de habitaciones   10. el elevador / el ascensor

9·9   **Horizontales** (*Across*)

3. impuesto   5. aerolínea   6. pasaje   7. registrarse   10. cabina   12. lugar   13. imprimir   16. bono   17. turbulencia

Verticales (*Down*)

1. aterrizar   2. huésped   4. tren   8. tripulación   9. buen viaje   11. preparativo   14. caber   15. fila   16. baño

9·10   1. equipaje   2. litera   3. mapa   4. oficina de cambios   5. no fumar   6. tarjeta de turista   7. aduana   8. cancelación   9. asiento   10. reserva electrónica   11. guía turística   12. autostop   13. salida

La palabra vertical: el montacargas (*freight elevator*)

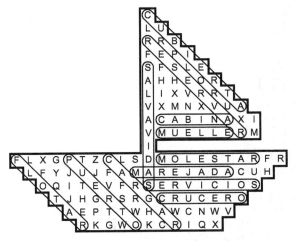

Words: servicios, reservar, cabina, crucero, cubierta, molestar, muelle, flotar, salvavidas, cargar, puerto, marejada

10 El tiempo libre, la diversión y el entretenimiento · *Free time, fun, and entertainment*

10·1 1. la orquesta 2. el piano 3. la flauta 4. contemporáneo 5. el jazz 6. el rock 7. el tango 8. el ritmo 9. el cubismo 10. el mueso 11. el poema 12. el judo 13. el club 14. el karate 15. el océano 16. la autobiografía 17. la guitarra eléctrica 18. el rugby 19. la canoa 20. la biografía 21. la fotografía 22. la discoteca 23. la novela de horror 24. el surfing 25. el camping 26. el sándwich 27. el restaurante 28. la tapa 29. el menú 30. el basquetbol

10·2 1. cocinar 2. la casa móvil 3. la tienda de campaña 4. la bici; la bicicleta 5. la ensalada 6. el refresco 7. la barbacoa 8. el documental 9. la estrella de cine 10. la tarjeta de crédito 11. flotar 12. la cerveza 13. la cuenta 14. el primer plato 15. el postre 16. la bebida 17. el plato 18. la comedia 19. el agua 20. el vino 21. caminar 22. servir 23. la heladería 24. la limonada 25. la porción 26. el precio 27. picante 28. la propina 29. el plan 30. dar la propina

10·3 1. b 2. c 3. a 4. d 5. a

10·4 1. to have a good time 2. joke 3. amusement park 4. children's literature 5. computer games 6. comic book store 7. to draw 8. toy 9. teen fiction 10. to go dancing 11. auditorium 12. to play an instrument 13. to sing 14. to laugh 15. plot

10·5 1. la taquilla 2. el acomodador 3. el submarino 4. el saco de dormir 5. el esmoquin 6. la edición de bolsillo 7. la batería 8. el lienzo 9. el casino 10. la escultura

10·6 1. entretenerse 2. canturrear 3. descansar 4. deslizarse 5. monopatín 6. videojuego 7. bailar 8. canción 9. dramático 10. premio 11. fracaso 12. conmovedor 13. estreno 14. escenario 15. subtítulo

10·7 1. leyenda 2. aplauso 3. lanzar 4. indicador 5. taquilla 6. emocionante 7. relajarse 8. argumento 9. televisión 10. usar 11. resistencia 12. acampar

La palabra vertical: la literatura (*literature*)

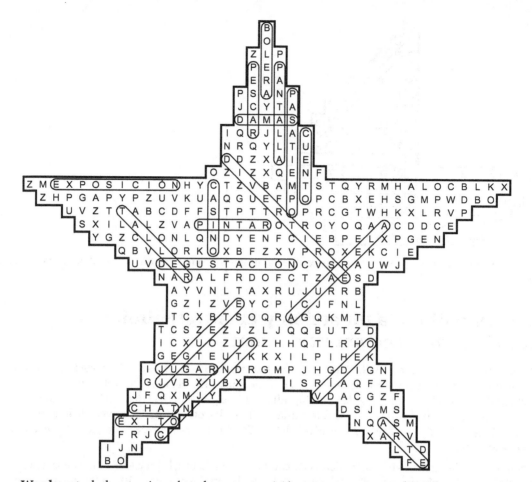

Words: arte, bolera, casino, chat, damas, exposición, pescar, conjunto, divertirse, pasatiempo, pintar, jugar, pantalla, cuento, taller, éxito, juguete, vídeo, acuarela, degustación

10·9 *Answers may vary.* 1. la videocámara 2. el cine / la televisión / la computadora / la computadora portátil 3. la taquilla / el servicio por Internet 4. los subtítulos 5. la galería de arte / el museo 6. el gimnasio 7. la cancha de tenis 8. el campo de golf 9. la mochila 10. la crema con filtro solar

10·10 *Answers will vary.* 1. What do I put on the floor to do exercises on? 2. What is a good way to safely build fitness? 3. What is a hiker? 4. Where can we find a gymnastics trainer? 5. Do you have the address for horseback riding? 6. Is there a place to ice skate? 7. Do you have a suggestion for where to buy shoes for jogging? 8. What are those people doing on that snowy hill? 9. Where can we go jogging around here? 10. Do you want to come skiing this weekend? 11. What is your favorite outdoor sport? 12. Who is buying women's pants and roller skates? 13. Do you want to run with us? 14. Do you do body building? 15. Do you ever go bowling?

10·11 1. d. el retrato 2. b. el bote 3. d. el bate 4. a. el bronceador 5. b. el bañador 6. a. el tablero 7. d. la piscina 8. a. marcar puntos 9. a. la guitarra 10. a. los deportes

10·12 **Horizontales** (*Across*)

4. guión 5. muñeca 7. puzle 9. estreno 11. visitar 12. caricatura 14. ocio 15. ficción 18. canturrear 20. ensayo 21. risa 22. lienzo 23. voz

Verticales (*Down*)

1. broma 2. títere 3. final 6. coleccionar 8. estatua 10. divertirse 13. acomodador 16. conjunto 17. mochila 19. reserva

11 La educación · *Education*

11·1 1. el grado 2. la gramática 3. el vocabulario 4. la biología 5. el cálculo 6. la composición
7. la historia 8. la música 9. participar 10. el laptop 11. el clic 12. el examen
13. audiovisual 14. el máster 15. la anatomía 16. el kindergarten 17. la clase
18. el semestre 19. el diccionario 20. la universidad 21. la multimedia 22. el diploma
23. el micrófono 24. el programador 25. la geografía 26. las matemáticas 27. la psicología
28. la trigonometría 29. el laboratorio de computadoras 30. la telecomunicación

11·2 1. el arte 2. el libro 3. usar 4. la literatura 5. cargar 6. el monitor 7. el ratón
8. el número 9. participar 10. imprimir 11. dibujar 12. la cerámica 13. el mapa
14. la impresora 15. el programa 16. la lectura 17. escanear 18. el escáner 19. la escuela /
el colegio 20. las tijeras 21. la pantalla 22. las vacaciones 23. escribir 24. el ensayo
25. el teclado 26. digital

11·3 1. a. enseñar 2. d. deletrear 3. c. la beca 4. b. el director 5. d. la asistencia
6. a. el horario 7. a. la materia 8. b. la lectura 9. c. la biblioteca 10. c. el sitio

11·4 1. a 2. b 3. d 4. c 5. b

11·5 1. el borrador 2. la biblioteca 3. el trabajo en equipo 4. la mochila 5. el diccionario
6. el cuaderno y el lápiz 7. el sacapuntas 8. el resaltador 9. la impresora
10. el programa antivirus

11·6 1. el títere 2. la mochila 3. la disertación 4. la biblioteca 5. la gorra 6. el diploma
7. el cuento de hadas 8. la publicidad 9. el secretariado 10. multimedia

11·7 1. aprender 2. gramática 3. debate 4. explicar 5. máster 6. videoconferencia
7. dibujar 8. tiza 9. discusión 10. profesora 11. responder 12. enseñar 13. mejorar
14. vacaciones 15. sustituto

11·8 1. literatura 2. asistencia 3. pizarra 4. universidad 5. bolígrafo 6. lápiz
7. interactiva 8. contar 9. ingresar 10. diploma 11. aprobado 12. dotado
La palabra vertical: la publicidad (*advertising*)

11·9

```
O R T O G R A F I A Y G J D F
Q U R A I C A H P E U X M K Q
N F W D F U M T E Q M D T I O
W A U R I C U L A R U B E W S
O I L F H V S L E E R K C M U
X P L Y T M E R Q H B O L L R
M M N I K J I R O D I S A O O
R E S A L T A D O R M O D M X
R P Z U S E S V A U I A Q A C
D W W I U M J R S R R U I T I
R L S Q M U O Y A R I R S E N
O A O K H W U O A O N J R I C
S L P Z D B S B A M O J G I C
B T N K E U H D E H N F X A I
A Q C J M J Y M P B C E A Z A
```

Words: asistir, bloquear, auricular, borrador, resaltador, tecla, memoria, módem, leer, horario, ciencia, ortografía, materia, usuario

11·10 1. literatura 2. aula 3. matricularse 4. habilidad 5. entender 6. impresora
7. promedio 8. calificar 9. pantalla
La palabra vertical: la materia (*subject*)

11·11 **Horizontales** (*Across*)

1. copiar 4. obedecer 5. aprender 7. deletrear 10. física 13. campana 14. deber
15. subrayar 17. biblioteca 19. maestro

Verticales (*Down*)

1. conferencia 2. resaltar 3. graduación 6. error 8. difícil 9. matemáticas
11. semestre 12. educación 16. beca 18. leer

11·12

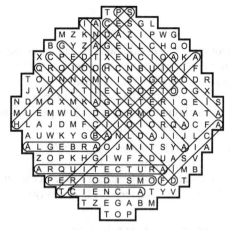

Words: contabilidad, álgebra, anatomía, arquitectura, biología, cálculo, química, ingeniería, geometría, historia, humanidades, periodismo, física, psicología, ciencia, trigonometría

12 Los trabajos y el negocio · *Occupations and business*

12·1
1. el/la turista   2. la agenda   3. el contrato   4. el sector   5. la visa   6. el jet   7. la seguridad
8. la asociación   9. el / la dentista   10. el farmacéutico / la farmacéutica   11. protestar
12. el veterinario   13. practicar   14. la ingeniería   15. la reportera   16. el golf   17. el/la piloto
18. la corporación   19. la solución   20. la protesta   21. el record   22. el compromiso
23. la experiencia   24. el doctor / la doctora   25. la pensión   26. el candidato   27. el/la
artista   28. el interés   29. la especuladora   30. atlético / atlética

12·2
1. ganar   2. la salida de emergencia   3. abrocharse   4. el capitán   5. la salida   6. el enfermero / la
enfermera   7. el banco   8. el trabajo   9. la policía   10. el cirujano / la cirujana
11. la escultura   12. la biblioteca   13. pintar   14. la sicóloga   15. la joya   16. el asiento
17. el cinturón de seguridad   18. la velocidad   19. la ventana   20. parquear   21. el anestesiólogo / la
anestesióloga   22. la electricidad   23. bailar   24. el autor / la autora   25. el editor / la
editora   26. el/la agente de viajes   27. el teatro   28. el préstamo   29. la comedia   30. la pintura

12·3
1. c   2. d   3. a   4. c   5. b

12·4
1. cosmetic surgery   2. unemployment   3. vacancy   4. holiday   5. automobile race
6. butcher   7. license   8. shareholder   9. pay raise   10. cook   11. Social Security   12. driver

12·5
1. corresponsal   2. seguro   3. bibliotecario   4. escultor   5. banquero   6. editora
7. músico   8. caricaturista   9. pediatra   10. panadero   11. jardinero   12. vendedora
13. intérprete   14. publicidad   15. periodismo

12·6
1. la bancarrota   2. los ascensos   3. el albañil   4. el panadero   5. el despido   6. la escultora
7. el anestesista   8. la jardinería   9. el urólogo   10. el sindicato

12·7

```
O A Q U T S S E Q P D C W E O I U
W X J S F P S I G E R E N T E K N
M U F W C S Q S J S A S T R E G W
R H L F L R R Z D M M N O Q F Z F
I I Y F W A N L C Y A C K Z U X C
E L E C T R I C I S T A E Y B M E
P S V E O C R P M U S G E G T C O
F O I J E N I O J W R E U I N C O
L Z R F K Q G C R G O H E Q M M
B L C T U H U I F O G J I Y E
A A O B E I L H E E K A T H F X D
K R N H L R A M C A N T A N T E I
U U B Q U I A T A J I B B R O A
N S I U J Y Z R D U D S O B W N
W M V R T E T Q Y A O F E T Y L T
G I S G E R R V D F V R Z V A H E
O F I C I O O J K P A A B Z D Z
```

Words: agente, banquero, comediante, electricista, filmadora, portera, higienista, juez, gerente, dramaturgo, siquiatra, cantante, sastre, oficio, árbitro

214   Answer key

12·8
1. el oncólogo / la oncóloga   2. el estado de cuentas   3. el cajero automático   4. el/la intérprete
5. el oftalmólogo / la oftalmóloga   6. la cuenta de ahorro   7. el/la dentista   8. el préstamo
9. el camarero / la camarera   10. el mecánico, la mecánica

12·9
1. el ciclismo   2. la técnica   3. el obrero   4. el empleo   5. el campeón   6. la relojera
7. el saldo   8. la entrevista   9. la huelguista   10. el empleado   11. la carrera de autos
12. la cuenta corriente   13. el presupuesto   14. la subasta   15. la campeona

12·10
1. liquidar   2. agente   3. músicos   4. obstetra   5. neurocirujano   6. editora   7. directora
8. arquitectura

La respuesta vertical: la moneda (*currency*)

12·11   **Horizontales** (*Across*)

2. renuncia   6. cita   7. ganancia   8. pérdida   10. gerente   12. anunciante   13. competir
14. sueldo   15. cuenta   16. accionista   18. depositar

Verticales (*Down*)

1. huelga   3. ganadora   4. depósito   5. entrenarse   6. campeonato   9. acuerdo
11. emplear   13. cajero   14. seguro   17. copa

13 El gobierno, la sociedad y las relaciones internacionales · *Government, society, and international relations*

13·1
1. el capitalismo   2. la república   3. la burocracia   4. la nación   5. comunista   6. la democracia
7. la región   8. el origen   9. la nación   10. socialista   11. atacar   12. la libertad   13. la sentencia
14. la minoría   15. el/la detective   16. la constitución   17. la discriminación   18. el candidato /
la candidata   19. democrático / democrática   20. el racismo   21. el/la inmigrante   22. la asamblea
23. legal   24. la intolerancia   25. inocente   26. la evidencia   27. la prisión   28. el testimonio
29. el veredicto   30. la sanción

13·2   1. V   2. V   3. F   4. V   5. F   6. V   7. F   8. F   9. F   10. F

13·3   1. c   2. a   3. c   4. d   5. d

13·4
1. el ladrón   2. el secuestro   3. la víctima   4. el vandalismo   5. la asesina   6. falsificar
7. el desfalco   8. la intervención   9. el pacto   10. el fraude   11. el gángster   12. asesinar
13. el homicidio   14. la estafa   15. el testigo   16. la autoridad   17. la dictadura   18. la patria
19. la alianza   20. votar   21. la coalición

13· 5
1. el embajador / la embajadora   2. el desertor / la desertora   3. el pacifismo   4. el/la cónsul
5. el desarme   6. la Organización de las Naciones Unidas   7. la guerra civil   8. el ultimátum
9. bombardear   10. el tratado internacional

13·6   1. las gorras   2. los convictos   3. el ladrón   4. la bandera   5. la muerte   6. el explosivo
7. un ilegal   8. la pistola negra   9. los alabañiles   10. la peluquería

13·7

```
V M R C U K D K H U D N J O T J S Q K
V O F F U Y U K Y Q U W D D B Q T K U
I K Z D A N F R R M U E N D V E R F C
Z X C E V I C T O R I A O B D I E F M
S F W A O Y C L B M O R C Z H X X P G
M J J E B W R T Z G E O N X A N P Z J
Z Q J A X L W B E B D H K L T L A Y
C U R N N R O U M D M J L Q Z H O L A
I E S Y X D F O A Q L Z G O D M S B O
U I T I A U B L O X Y E X Q U O I W D
D Z O G M X S P S A D K Y D D Y V G Q
A X O K O R C H R I F P T R B N O W Y
D B Y U B P C W N E V E E X F T F T R
A X H P Q O A Y E I J U P G S E O A H
N O Q H W P M C Q S S C U I A C S L N E
A F U V T P L B U A W X I M N T J Q R
V K C C K R K T A S G P C C U B U I
Z X V D E V M I A G A O M I G C E R
A L C A L D E W D M X R P K N O Z O V
```

Words: acusar, bomba, ciudadana, explosivo, miedo, fuego, bombero, abogado, alcalde, pánico, prejuicio, tanque, acuerdo, victoria, testigo, herir

13·8 1. elegir 2. líder 3. asamblea 4. cadena perpetua 5. ejército 6. revólver 7. coalición 8. autoridades 9. monarquía 10. inspector 11. explosivo 12. naturalización 13. testificar 14. oposición

La respuesta vertical: el acercamiento (*reconciliation*)

13·9 1. extranjera 2. absolver 3. inmigración 4. ministro 5. culpable 6. naturalización 7. presunto 8. huellas 9. notaria 10. condenar

La palabra vertical: el impuesto (*tax*)

13·10 1. emigrante 2. conservador 3. independiente 4. deportación 5. permiso 6. culpabilidad 7. apelar 8. inocencia 9. sentenciar 10. incendio 11. chantaje 12. artillería 13. estafa 14. víctima 15. infantería

13·11 1. respetar 2. declararse 3. batallón 4. pacifista 5. división 6. destruir 7. armamento 8. poder 9. traición 10. capturar 11. equipo médico 12. sabotaje 13. saquear 14. disparar 15. marina

13·12 **Horizontales** (*Across*)

1. delincuencia 5. rendirse 8. investigación 10. abstenerse 12. testificar 15. explotar 16. traumática 17. milicia 18. miedo

Verticales (*Down*)

2. contribuyente 3. hostilidad 4. seguridad 6. juramento 7. ultimátum 9. opositora 11. diputado 13. imputar 14. pánico

14 El mundo y la naturaleza · *The world and nature*

14·1 1. irreversible 2. nuclear 3. el tractor 4. el hámster 5. global 6. el/la astronauta 7. el cometa 8. el atlas 9. la fauna 10. la flora 11. el tornado 12. el cosmos 13. el eclipse 14. el meteoro 15. el planeta 16. el huracán 17. el tsunami 18. la iguana 19. continental 20. variable 21. biodegradable 22. el hábitat 23. el poni 24. el koala 25. el/la ecologista 26. la lava 27. el canal 28. el quetzal 29. la boa 30. el cardinal

14·2 1. la frontera 2. el lago 3. el océano 4. el país 5. la región 6. la isla 7. la bahía 8. el golfo 9. el mar 10. la alergia 11. la basura 12. la reserva 13. el pollo 14. la cucaracha 15. volar 16. el pato / la pata 17. el cerdo 18. el pavo 19. el pez 20. los guantes

14·3 1. b 2. a 3. d 4. c 5. b

14·4 1. el cerdo 2. el gallo 3. el caballo 4. la vaca 5. el pato / la pata 6. el pollo 7. el conejo, la coneja 8. el pavo 9. la serpiente 10. la rana

14·5 1. la cascada 2. el rinoceronte 3. el agua potable 4. derretir 5. las vacas 6. los lobos 7. la manguera 8. el tiburón 9. el efecto invernadero 10. la perturbación

14·6 1. el aire 2. la atmósfera 3. el astro 4. el cosmos 5. la órbita 6. el frío 7. la nube 8. el fresco 9. la galaxia 10. la luna 11. el oxígeno 12. el satélite 13. gravitar 14. el universo 15. espacial 16. la ingravidez 17. la rotación 18. helar 19. ventoso 20. la avalancha

14·7 1. llovizna 2. arena 3. superficie 4. cráter 5. orilla 6. navegable 7. despejada 8. insecticida 9. colina 10. inundación 11. olivo 12. naturaleza 13. ecosistema 14. selva

La palabra vertical: las condiciones (*conditions*)

14·8 1. acantilado 2. paisaje 3. península 4. altitud 5. meseta 6. arroyo 7. terrestre 8. rocosa 9. manantial 10. corriente 11. torrente 12. nublado 13. glaciar 14. aguacero 15. escarcha

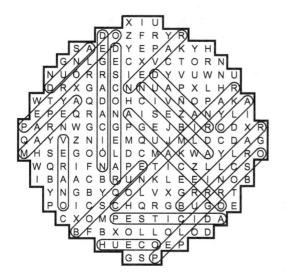

Words: dañar, degradación, duna, niebla, bosque, peligroso, hueco, petróleo, pesticida, contaminar, brillar, aguacero, nevar, verano, descongelar, marea, ola

14·10   1. el cortacésped   2. el irrigador, la manguera   3. el abono   4. los agricultores   5. la tierra
6. la cosecha   7. el jardín   8. pacer en los campos   9. los criadores   10. los árboles frutales

14·11   *Answers may vary.*   1. En el Océano Ártico y también en el Caribe.   2. En el reciclaje.
3. Es la abundancia de muchos productos naturales.   4. Los defensores del ambiente.
5. No, son animales domésticos.   6. No, son insectos.   7. Es un zumbido.   8. Es la mariposa.
9. El clavel, el narciso y la margarita.   10. La contaminación.

14·12   1. la cueva   2. la roca   3. el deshielo   4. el arado   5. soleado   6. fértil   7. el calor
8. crecer   9. irrigar   10. la oveja   11. la rana   12. el injerto   13. el rastrillo

La palabra vertical: las estaciones (*the seasons*)

14·13   **Horizontales** (*Across*)

1. subida   4. temperatura   6. sequía   7. destrucción   10. sombra   11. efecto invernadero
14. tronar   15. cometa   18. acantilado   19. derrame

Verticales (*Down*)

2. ingravidez   3. amanecer   5. cambio   8. río   9. constelación   11. extinción   12. astro
13. erosionar   16. bajar   17. valle

15   Los números, las cantidades, y el tiempo · *Numbers, quantities, and time*

15·1   1. el número   2. la suma   3. el total   4. la yarda   5. el doble   6. el área   7. la división
8. el kilogramo   9. cero   10. el kilómetro   11. el doble   12. la capacidad   13. la hora
14. la dimensión   15. gigantesco   16. calcular   17. el litro   18. la diferencia   19. el centímetro
20. el metro

15·2   1. la caja   2. el número   3. la superficie   4. la mañana   5. la taza   6. la cucharada
7. la cucharadita   8. mucho   9. el día   10. la dirección   11. la contraseña   12. la receta
13. el domingo   14. la fecha   15. la noche   16. julio   17. el amanecer   18. el mes   19. mañana
20. junio   21. agosto   22. el juego de cartas   23. el cumpleaños   24. la milla

15·3   1. c   2. a   3. b   4. d   5. a

15·4   1. a las doce en punto   2. da la hora   3. sumar   4. pesar toneladas   5. las pulgadas
6. computar   7. cardinales   8. la medianoche   9. la mitad   10. siete

15·5   1. la geometría   2. el álgebra   3. la millonaria   4. el ángulo   5. bastante   6. pocos
7. unas cuantas   8. un poco   9. mucho   10. más   11. pequeño   12. tantas   13. tanta
14. algunos   15. el cuarto

15·6 1. en punto 2. los meses 3. pesar 4. ocho 5. rombo 6. cuarto 7. enero 8. noviembre 9. tarjeta de banco 10. anoche 11. jueves 12. ejercicio

La respuesta vertical: el porcentaje (*percentage*)

15·7 1. calculadora 2. catorce 3. anteayer 4. hoy 5. fin de semana 6. febrero 7. año 8. mañana por la mañana 9. doblar 10. treinta y uno 11. bocado 12. semana 13. noviembre 14. cien mil 15. marzo

15·8 1. la báscula 2. el calendario 3. la tarjeta de cumpleaños 4. la calculadora 5. medida en pulgadas 6. la rebanada 7. la cucharadita 8. la geometría 9. la casilla 10. la tarjeta de banco y la identidad

15·9

Words: botella, calculadora, diciembre, profunda, dividir, división, enorme, casilla, millonario, número, onza, contraseña, pedazo, restar

15·10 **Horizontales** (*Across*)

1. puñado 8. casilla 9. bocado 10. geometría 11. quince 13. capacidad 15. pasado mañana 17. cuatro

Verticales (*Down*)

2. anteayer 3. contraseña 4. pesar 5. libra 6. profundidad 7. madrugada 12. pedazo 14. añadir 16. sexta